THE MIGHTY GODDESS

WORLD MYTHS

STORIES
Sally Pomme CLAYTON

PAPERCUTS
Sophie HERXHEIMER

The History Press

For my sister, and all our sisters. SPC

For my daughter, and all our daughters. SH

First published 2023

The History Press
97 St George's Place, Cheltenham,
Gloucestershire, GL50 3QB
www.thehistorypress.co.uk

Text © Sally Pomme Clayton, 2023
Illustrations © Sophie Herxheimer, 2023

The right of Sally Pomme Clayton to be identified as the
Author of this work has been asserted in accordance with the
Copyright, Designs and Patents Act 1988.

British Library Cataloguing in Publication Data.
A catalogue record for this book is available from the British Library.

ISBN 978 0 7509 9617 4

Typesetting and origination by The History Press
Designed by Jemma Cox
Printed and bound in Great Britain by TJ Books Limited, Padstow, Cornwall.

Trees for Life

Contents

Journey of the Goddess   6

CREATOR   11

Maiden of the Air, Mother of the Water – *Finland*   12
Grandmother Spider – *Hopi, Southwestern*
    United States of America   15
Sun Woman – *Aboriginal and Torres Strait*
    Islander Peoples, Northern Territory, Australia   18
Nut, Sky Goddess – *Egypt*   21
Garden Goddess – *Dinka, Sudan*   24
Sedna, Goddess of the Sea – *Inuit, Arctic*   27
Saule Shining One – *Lithuania/Latvia*   32
Primal Mother of the Deep – *Mesopotamia*   34
Saraswati, Creator of Creation – *India*   38

VIRGIN   41

Vesta Virgin Flame – *Roman*   42
Arianrhod – *Wales*   46
Changing Woman – *Navajo,*
    Southwestern United States of America   49
Being Bears for Artemis – *Greece*   52
Fair Maid of February – *Ireland*   58
Idunn's Apples – *Scandinavia*   61
Morning Star, Evening Star – *Lithuania/Latvia*   65
Goddess of the Hunt – *Roman*   68
Maiden, Mother of All – *Christian*   73

WARRIOR   79

Battle of Day and Night – *Sumeria*   80
Pele, Volcano Goddess – *Hawaii*   83
Mistress of Magic, Speaker of Spells – *Egypt*   88
Anahita – *Iran*   92
Durga Demon-Slayer – *India*   94
Pallas Athena – *Greece*   99
Amaterasu Sun Goddess – *Japan*   103
Sekhmet Lioness – *Egypt*   109
Lilith, Goddess of Night – *Hebrew*   111

LOVER 117

Aphrodite, Foam Born – *Greece* 118
Sisters in Love and Death – *Mesopotamia* 120
The Net of Venus – *Roman* 129
Freyja, Goddess of Sex – *Scandinavia* 133
Chang'e, Lady of the Moon – *China* 138
Aphrodite and Anchises – *Greece* 141
Isis and Osiris – *Egypt* 145
Erzulie Freda – *Vodou, Haiti* 153
Venus and Adonis – *Roman* 156

MOTHER 159

Pachamama – *Inca, Andes* 160
Cybele, Magna Mater – *Roman* 162
Oshun, Sweet Water – *Yoruba, Nigeria* 167
Green Tara – *Tibet* 171
Demeter and Persephone – *Greece* 176
Queen Mother of the West – *China* 185
The Seven Scorpions of Isis – *Egypt* 189
Lakshmi, Mother of Prosperity – *India* 193

CRONE 197

Asase Yaa, Old Woman Earth – *Ashanti, Ghana* 198
Baba Marta – *Bulgaria* 200
Great Lady of the Night – *Māori, New Zealand* 202
Fortuna – *Roman* 206
Cihuacóatl, Snake Woman – *Aztec, Mexico* 208
Cailleach – *Ireland* 210
Elli, Old Age – *Scandinavia* 214
Hekate, Goddess of the Three Ways – *Greece* 217

Bibliography 220
Acknowledgements 222
Thanks 223

Journey of the Goddess

The goddess has multiple forms that resonate across the world in one mighty being. The oldest images of the goddess were carved in bone and stone around 40,000 years ago. Myths of the goddess appear and reappear in multiple versions and are both universal and local, containing motifs that are shared by all, while taking cultural and geographically specific forms. These myths are a precious hoard that echo from eternity down into our deepest selves. By bringing these global goddesses together I hope to honour these diverse stories, allowing their images and narratives to reverberate with each other, revealing our shared cultural roots and collective preoccupations. But her myths come with a warning – these stories have not been tamed! They are about lust and greed, rape and rage, death and destruction, jealousy and murder, transformation and rebirth. I have not softened the content but respected it and responded to it, exploring some of its many meanings.

The goddess repeatedly inhabits particular roles, frequently appearing as creator, virgin, warrior, lover, mother, and crone. This book follows the journey of the goddess from creator to crone, and her manifestations in these roles across the world. I have chosen to define the goddess as a supreme deity who is, or was, worshipped. The divine goddess appears as female, both male and female, or transcends gender.

I have also chosen to focus on myth rather than fairy tale. Powerful characters, such as Baba Yaga, who have goddess aspects but appear in fairy tales, have not been included – forgive me Baba! Myths and fairy tales have distinct and very different structural patterns. Myth has tangents and back stories, like a family tree that spreads outwards. It has many possible routes through its narratives, with open beginnings and endings. It is linked to ritual and worship, and usually the narratives connect to a wider pantheon of gods and goddess and their stories.

This book is my version of the images and narratives of the one and multiple goddess. I have taken my own journey through the myths, placing the goddess at the centre of each story, not at the side or lost at the end where she often can be. I have sometimes chosen to leave out male characters or reduce their roles – there are plenty of collections where you can find their stories! By telling the myths from the point of view of the goddess I discovered new emotions, meanings and metaphoric realities.

I have been performing many of these myths for nearly forty years: starting as a young storyteller, feeling as though I was not equal to the material, trying to discover how I could bring ancient myths to contemporary audiences, both honouring the material and giving it new life. I continue this exploration. The myths in this collection arose from extensive research, finding multiple versions, looking at artefacts and locations, then weaving my own versions from sometimes disparate fragments of story and history that might not have been brought together before. Some of these versions have also been shaped through repeated performances and by the responses of audiences across the UK and beyond. Audiences help a storyteller find rhythms and patterns in the narrative, they inspire jokes and humour and bring out the drama and characters in a story. This book is a legacy to a life of living with, loving, and performing these myths.

All these myths were once spoken or chanted, some still are. Some of the myths exist as 'urtexts' – an earliest version, written on stone walls, clay tablets, papyrus or palm leaf. Most of the myths exist as multiple written versions, collected and transcribed or developed from oral sources, turned into books, translated, made into operas and films, rewritten, then turned back into performances on street corners. I continue this endless process.

I have been shocked to find how little narrative exists for some goddesses. Their stories are absent from even recent collections. I have found that goddesses who are part of major pantheons tend to have more narrative, more has been collected and written down, and more artefacts linked to them exist. While local or household goddesses who are on the edges of pantheons have less narrative, less has been written down and less remains. These goddesses were, and some still are, part of private rituals rather than public worship, they might have important shrines in the home or local landscape, but their lower status seems to mean less has passed from oral to written traditions. I hope their stories will be collected for future generations. For some goddesses very little narrative exists, instead there might be potent images, a few prayers or rituals. Some of these goddesses are so important I wanted to include them here. I looked at statues, patterns on shards of pot, textiles, songs or prayers to find fragments of narrative. Examining what a goddess holds and wears, the gestures she makes, what blessings she confers and what she represents are all clues to her story. Goddesses usually have several epithets (names) that describe her energies and powers. Epithets are a feature of myths, repeated in prayers and praise songs, inscribed on shrines and objects. They are useful in discovering more about a goddess and I have included some of her multiple names to evoke her different attributes.

The goddess often appears in multiple roles, all at the same time, in one myth! I chose which section to place each myth, according to which role was the most dominant. In the 'Creator' myths, the goddess often appears in all roles simultaneously. Grandmother Spider is both creator and crone, who spins the world. Sedna is lover, mother, warrior, but, most of all, creator – all the sea creatures are born from her body. The 'Creator' myths often have a violent aspect, body parts are cut away, goddesses are destroyed, sky is separated from earth, light from darkness, water from earth, so that something can be born. While the myth of Tiamat, 'Primal Mother of the Deep', describes a cosmic battle between male and female power that ends with the goddess's own body becoming the Earth.

In the 'Virgin' myths the goddess often appears as a warrior, passionately choosing virginity, then fiercely defending it. Virgin goddesses often suffer rape and the loss of their precious virginity and then turn to righteous fury and warrior rage. Virgins Arianrhod, Changing Woman and Mary miraculously become mothers. Many of the virgin goddesses are linked to the education of young girls, passing on the values and skills of the virgin.

In the 'Warrior' myths the goddess is born from anger that flashes out of an eye, turning into Durga or Sekhmet. Athena is born from Zeus's head then goes to war with him. Goddesses Lilith and Isis both steal the unknown magic name of the 'father' god and gain ultimate power. The power and rage of these goddesses often cannot be stopped, as they defend their people, their land, the planet and the universe.

In the 'Lover' myths the goddess becomes creator, her desire and satisfaction spreading fertility across the world. In the myths of Isis, Ishtar and Venus dried sticks burst into blossom, bodies become flowers and trees. As a lover the goddess often becomes a warrior too. Lovers lose their beloved and undertake impossible quests and battles to get them back, while desire turns to vengeance for Freyja and Aphrodite.

In the 'Mother' myths the goddess is often the life-giving Earth itself. The mother goddess can also be a virgin, or eternally young, possessing the secret of immortal life. The mother merges with warrior as Isis furiously protects her son, and Demeter's search for her daughter turns into a curse that punishes the world. The mother goddess, Cybele, transcends gender and all roles, and I have honoured Cybele with no pronouns.

The 'Crone' myths link old age with both birth and death, the crone is a mother and her birth canal becomes a tomb. Goddesses Asase Yaa and Hine-nui-te-pō are midwives who cradle the dying soul like a baby, so it can be born again. The crone is also a virgin, giving birth to herself endlessly, as winter becomes spring. Both Mexican Cihuacóatl and Ashanti Asase Yaa are connected to snakes who shed their skin and give eternal life.

Look out for the sparks that flash between these myths! I still find it thrilling and mysterious that so many parallel images, motifs and narrative elements reappear again and again across different cultures, languages and continents. These ancient stories connect us all. You will meet some goddesses and pantheons more than once as the journey of the goddess continues through the collection. I hope this book is a resource that leads you to explore other versions, to find the bits of narrative I have left out, and seek out the many, many other goddess myths I have not told here.

In goddess myths across the world humans often make the same great mistake: they do not recognise the goddess, and they are punished for it, losing the goddess's blessing and gifts. So, keep alert, the Mighty Goddess is everywhere and in us all. May her images and narratives give us courage, inspiration, and hope.

CREATOR

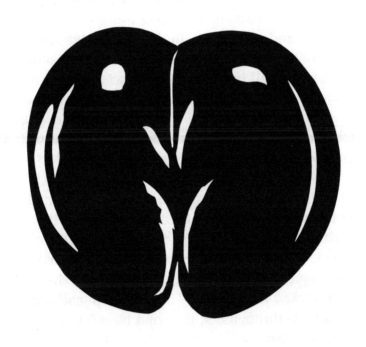

Maiden of the Air, Mother of the Water

Finland

Forever has always existed. Darkness was always there. And the sea and sky were there too. There was no earth yet or light, just dark sky and rolling sea. In that time there was one girl, one girl all alone. She was Ilmater, Airess, Maiden of the Air. She lived by herself in the smooth, spacious fields of the air. The Wide-Wandering Goddess blew this way and that. For a long time, Airess played in the open meadows of the sky. Then she got bored, something was lacking. Ilmater was all alone and there was nothing for her to rest her feet on!

The Maiden of the Air swooped down and landed on the billows below. Ilmater floated on the empty sea, drifted on dark water without end. Then a blast of wind circled Ilmater. It was a hot wind, a lusty wind and it wrapped around her, pulled her close and squeezed her tight. The wind raised the sea into a foam and rocked the maiden. The wind kept rocking the girl. The wind blew through her, the wind blew into her, the wind blew Ilmater pregnant.

Maiden of the Air became Mother of the Water. She swam through the sea looking for land. She swam north, swam south, swam east, swam west. She was looking for a place to rest, looking for somewhere to give birth. There was nothing but water, no land, no home, nowhere to give birth. Ilmater floated in the darkness carrying her baby for a long time, a very long time. She swam across the sea for seven hundred years, seven hundred years passed and nothing was born.

Then a little bird came. It fluttered about looking for land. The bird flew north, flew south, flew east, flew west. The bird was looking for a place to rest, looking for somewhere to build her nest. There was nothing but water, no land, no home, nowhere to lay her egg. The lonely mother knew just how the bird felt so she raised her knee from the sea. The little bird saw something rise up out of the waves and thought it was a grassy hillock.

The bird swooped down and made her home on the knee of the Wide-Wandering Goddess. The bird pulled long strands of hair from Ilmater's head and wove them into a nest. And there she laid her egg. A golden egg!

The bird sat on the egg, brooded the egg, turned the egg, warmed the egg. The egg grew hot. Ilmater felt her knee warming, her skin smouldering, her blood boiling, her sinews scorching, her bones melting. She could not help herself, she twitched her knee and the egg fell into the sea. The egg cracked. The golden egg broke into bits, and the bits turned into beautiful things. The universe tumbled out. The egg shell became the land. The egg yolk glowed as the sun. The white of the egg gleamed palely as the moon. The spots on the egg became the clouds. The speckles on the egg became the stars. And so the world was made!

Ilmater pulled herself out of the sea onto dry land. At last Maiden of the Air had found a place to rest, Mother of the Water had a home. The Wide-Wandering Goddess could give birth. We are all the heirs of Airess and that first egg.

This creation myth is from the Finnish epic The Kalevala. *This poetic epic contains a series of spells, chants, myths, remedies and stories. It is sung as a duet between two singer-storytellers, one leads and the other follows repeating the last words and phrases. This repetition gives the performance an incantatory feeling.*

Grandmother Spider

Hopi, Southwestern
United States of America

Grandmother Spider thought, 'make something!' She was Thought Old Woman and whatever she thought came into being. She wove things out of nothing, pulling creation out of herself. She thought, 'Earth is empty, silent, still.' Grandmother Spider's thoughts fluttered. She thought of green. She scooped up mud with her slender fingers and spat on it. She mixed soil with saliva and formed her thoughts into the shapes of trees. She thought of orange and blue and shaped birds. She thought of brown and white and formed crawling creatures. She moulded her thoughts into existence and laid the shapes out on the muddy ground. The shapes were silent and still.

Grandmother Spider began to spin, twirling her pointed fingers so silvery threads appeared. She wove lacy capes from her threads, fleecy and soft as clouds. She covered each shape with a white cape, wrapping the shapes in her web of existence. Then she began to sing, murmuring the song of life. The shapes stirred, breathed, rustled, grew, croaked, growled, squealed, cooed, crawled, swam, ran, flew.

Grandmother Spider's thoughts flickered. She thought of hugging and holding hands, of laughter and song. She took more mud and formed human beings. She wrapped people in her life-giving capes and sang the song of creation over them. She gave humans beating hearts, breath and speech.

Grandmother Spider's thoughts trembled. She wove long, shimmering threads around the world and set Earth spinning. She tied the ends of the threads to the tallest trees with the deepest roots to hold Earth steady. And spiders have been fixing their webs to trees ever since. The world was alive. Earth was no longer empty, silent, still.

Grandmother Spider has been weaving our fates ever since. She stole fire to keep humans warm. She wove baskets and nets for hunting and carrying. She taught humans how to spin, weave and play string games. She showed the direction in which to turn the spindle so it follows Earth's rotation. And when Earth was overwhelmed with water and everything flooded Grandmother Spider wove a raft, a silver bridge so animals and humans were saved.

But most of all Thought Old Woman teaches us thought. How keeping the pattern in your mind as you write, draw, compose or weave will help it to appear. And Grandmother Spider is with you, if you just listen. She is hiding behind your ear, guiding you so that you reach the end of your journey. Thought Old Woman is always there, whispering her secret knowledge, showing us how to shape thought.

Stories of Grandmother Spider are found in the living myths and epics of many First Nations, especially in the south-west and along the west coast of North America. In the last paragraph the list of things that Grandmother Spider creates each have multiple versions of stories.

Sun Woman

Aboriginal and Torres Strait Islander Peoples,
Northern Territory, Australia

Wuriunpranilli makes a fire. Twigs smoulder and the first rays of dawn streak across the sky. She scrapes up red ochre, dips her finger into the dust and draws patterns across her body. She decorates herself with red dust, covers herself with red dots, red rays, red flames, red spirals, red circles. She cloaks herself in the land itself. The patterns begin to gleam, to move, to swirl and red ochre rises into the air. Red dust scatters and sparkles, becoming particles of light. The clouds turn red. The sunrise is on its way!

Wuriunpranilli twists bark into a torch and holds it to the fire. The torch catches and begins to burn. She lifts her torch high and sets off. Sun Woman walks up into the sky, her torch fills earth with light and she walks from east to west. Birds follow her, singing, calling up the morning. Her torch blazes as she journeys across the sky. It is burning hot at midday, then her fire fades and Sun Woman climbs down into the western horizon. She gathers twigs and lights a new fire. She scoops up red ochre and paints fresh patterns on her skin. Red dust rises, scattering, and the sky glows red. The sunset is on its way!

Birds stop singing, fluff up their feathers and go to sleep. But Wuriunpranilli does not sleep. She continues her journey. She clambers down a dark hole into a tunnel under the earth. She walks all night through the tunnel that connects west with east. She walks all the way back to her morning camp. And there Sun Woman lights her fire again and paints her body with spirals of blood and fire, circles of earth and air. In her endless cycle of rising and setting, living and dying, Sun Woman brings us all heat, light, life, forever.

Wuriunpranilli is a solar goddess who is part of the profound sacred mythologies and living traditions of the indigenous peoples of Australia. This is my interpretation inspired by several versions and the brilliant essay 'Australian Aboriginal Myth' by Isobel White and Helen Payne in The Feminist Companion to Mythology *edited by Carolyne Larrington.*

Nut, Sky Goddess

Egypt

Nut curves across space, her body arches up and over, as she balances on her fingertips and toes. Her body is sprinkled with stars. The Milky Way streams across her belly and breasts, along her arms, down her thighs and calves. The moon glitters in her hair. The Sky Goddess protects the world, all beneath are held in her embrace. Stretched out below is Geb, God of Earth. He lies on his side, one hand supporting his head the other hand resting on his knee. His body nurtures life. Forests grow from his thighs, mountains rise from his back, lakes flow from his lap, deserts spread across his shoulders.

Nut and Geb were created by Sun God Ra from his own potent semen, his own vigorous spit. The Sun God sails across Nut's body every day in his golden boat of a million years. Ra embarks early in the morning when he is just a small boy with golden hair. He sails across the Sky Goddess and by the middle of the day Ra has become a burning warrior. By the end of the day Ra is a trembling old man with bright white hair. Goddess Nut opens her mouth and swallows Ra. He continues his journey travelling through the night of Nut's body, through darkness to dawn. Then Nut gives birth to Ra. The Sun God is born again, a golden-haired baby. And the sky has been stained with the ruddy flood of Nut's afterbirth, the rosy glow of dawn, ever since.

Nut arched over Geb and was forever filled with desire. The Sky Goddess was eternally looking down on the God of Earth and was consumed by longing. Until she could resist him no longer. She waited until Ra was travelling though the dark of her body then slipped down to earth. She lay down on top of Geb, at last they held each other, embracing so tightly that nothing could come between them. Sky and Earth coupled and Nut conceived.

Nut's belly began to swell and Ra cursed her, 'I did not create you to couple. I did not create you to conceive. You will never give birth. Not on any day, of any week, of any month, of any year.' Nut's belly grew large and round and hard as stone. She howled in pain and her cries echoed across the universe. But she could not give birth, not on any day, week, month, year.

Thoth, God of Justice, scribe to the gods, with the head of a black ibis and curving beak, heard her cries. 'This is not justice,' he said. 'If Sun will not help, Moon will.'

Thoth knew Moon loved playing chess. He set up the board and arranged the pieces.

Moon glittered, 'Let's place bets,' she said. She was sure she would win. 'I will stake a tiny portion of my light.'

'Then I will give a drop of my wisdom,' said Thoth. The game began. Thoth played as if he was at war storming across the board mercilessly taking Moon's pieces one by one, pressing Moon to a murderous endgame. Then checkmate! Moon lost. Thoth collected his winnings, a sliver of moonlight.

The God of Justice carried the moonlight to Nut.

'This light does not belong to any day, of any week, of any month, of any year. Use it to give birth.'

In the silver light, the tiny slip of time, Nut gave birth. She was relieved of her great burden and gave birth to four children, two males, Osiris and Set, and two females, Isis and Nepthys. Nut had brought the four great gods of Egypt into being. But ever since then Moon has waxed and waned each month because she lost a tiny bit of her light and will never get it back.

Garden Goddess

Dinka, Sudan

Lush increase, green flourish, make our gardens grow Abuk. First Woman teach us how to dig and plant, to water and tend. Garden Goddess show us how to spread fertility across the world.

Abuk was there from the beginning when sky was so close to earth a rope connected the two realms. First Woman Abuk and First Man Garang could climb up the rope into the sky whenever they liked. They visited Sky God Nhialic and his infinite pile of seeds. Sky God would pick out a kernel of corn or a grain of millet and give first humans one seed each. Abuk and Garang would plant, harvest and grind their single stalk of grain. They took care when they were digging the ground or tending their tiny crop, because sky was so close to earth they did not want to strike the great Nhialic by accident.

There was barely enough food for two and when children were born the first family went hungry. Abuk raged, 'Sky God wants us to starve. Nhialic desires earth to be barren.'

Abuk was filled with grit. And the next time they climbed the rope, as Sky God gave First Man a grain of millet, Abuk bent and seized a handful of seeds and tucked them into her dress. This time she dug the ground deeper and wider and planted all her seeds. Corn grew, millet spread thick, green, golden. There would be enough food for them all.

Abuk raised her staff to harvest the crop, grit had produced goodness. She was so excited she forgot to take care of the sky. Her staff cut through corn and clouds, and struck Nhialic on his big toe!

The Sky God let out a cry, 'Curse you below!'
    Nhialic began to pull up the rope.
    'May you suffer pain just like me!'
    Nhialic kept on pulling up the rope, until sky was separated from earth. 'I leave you all down there, to die alone.'

Nhialic set the sky free, and it floated upwards, far away from earth. And the sky has been a long, very long way from earth ever since. And from that moment onwards all humans have suffered pain, and each one of us faces death on our own.

Abuk tilled the soil, watered and tended her crops. Her harvest was abundant and she fed her family. After the harvest Abuk collected the seeds and named each one for the future. Abuk gave her seeds to the world so that life would continue. Then she taught her children the skills of cultivation.

The ancestors of Abuk wove stalks of wheat into a crown, decorating it with fragrant flowers and placed it on Abuk's head. 'Garden Goddess spread green across the world. Abuk make our gardens grow in plots and pots, windowsills and allotments, backyards and tubs, parks and commons, fields and furrows. Garden Goddess make lush increase, green flourish, spread fertility across the world.'

Versions of this myth are found in many countries and cultures across Africa, especially in Nigeria and Ghana. One version includes the Goddess Asase Yaa.

Sedna,
Goddess of the Sea

Inuit, Arctic

Sedna gave birth to the sea creatures from her body. They are her children, she cares for them and calls us to care too.

In the beginning the ocean was empty and there were no sea creatures. In those days Sedna lived by the icy sea with her five brothers. She had long black plaits, rosy cheeks and many suitors. She refused them all. No one matched her brothers. Sedna spent the summer hunting moose and caribou alongside her brothers, and when winter came feasted with them beside the fire. When the meat ran out, there were no fish to catch, and so they would often go hungry until spring.

One day Raven flew across the world looking for a wife. His beady eyes spied Sedna. 'She is for me!' Raven – shapeshifter, trickster, god, king – fluttered his wings and there stood a man with raven black hair, reindeer skin boots and a parka of white wolverine fur. He looked at his reflection in the sea. 'Tasty,' he preened. 'Except the eyes.'

His eyes were still beady bird's eyes. Raven stamped his foot and a pair of snow-goggles appeared made of white bone with a tiny slit for each eye. He put them on.

'She'll never know,' he squawked. Then he called up a canoe and paddled across the bay.

Sedna was cutting up meat with her silver crescent-shaped knife. She heard the splash of paddle in water but did not look up. Raven got out of the canoe, tapped his boot on the ground and gave a slow whistle. Sedna raised her eyes and saw something so splendid her heart flipped. She had never felt that before.

'I'm the king,' crooned Raven. 'In love with me yet?'

Sedna put down her knife and rose to her feet in a daze. She did not call to her brothers, she just climbed into the canoe. Raven charmed her, flattered her, put such a spell of seduction upon her, by the time they crossed the bay she was in love. So in love, when Raven unfurled two black wings and carried her through the air she thought it was a passionate embrace. So in love, she thought his nest was a castle with many rooms.

So in love, the salt sting spray of the sea seemed like a warm fire. So much in love, raw meat tasted roasted.

Until a gust of wind blew Raven's snow-goggles off. Sedna saw the beady bird's eyes and the spell was broken. She looked about and saw that she was sitting in a nest and her husband had claws, wings and a beak. 'Help! Brothers!' she shouted.

Raven circled the nest, cawing to calm his wife. Sedna shouted louder. 'Help, my brothers! I married a bird!'

Her cries carried across the water, and her brothers leapt into a canoe and followed their sister's voice. Raven flapped and croaked but Seda would not stop crying. Raven soared away to fetch meat to soothe her. Sedna's brothers arrived and saw their sister sitting in a nest on top of a cliff. 'I married a bird!' she sobbed.

Her eldest brother scrambled up the cliff, lifted Sedna into his arms and carried her down into the canoe. Her brothers were paddling away when a shadow fell on the boat.

'Give her back!' croaked Raven.

The huge bird flapped his wings and beat the wind into a storm. Waves crashed over the side of the canoe, washing Sedna into the sea. She sank down under the water. She could see the boat above her and swam up and clung onto the side of the canoe with her hands. Raven circled overhead, 'She's mine!'

Raven beat his wings and the boat rocked from side to side. The eldest brother cried, 'We must give her back, or we'll die!'

The brothers lifted their paddles and brought them down onto Sedna's fingers. Her hands were so cold her fingertips snapped off and tumbled into the sea. As her fingertips touched the water they turned into fishes and swam away. Sedna clung onto the canoe with her knuckles. Her brothers brought their paddles down and her knuckles snapped off, tumbled into the sea, turned into seals and swam away. Sedna clung on with the stumps of her fingers. Her brothers brought their paddles down hard, the stumps snapped off, turned into walrus and swam away. Sedna clung on with her two thumbs. Her brothers brought their paddles down and her thumbs snapped off, turned into two great whales and swam away. Sedna could cling on no more, and sank down under the waves. Raven's bride was gone, and he flew away. The storm vanished and the brothers were safe. But they paddled home alone, they had lost their sister forever.

The sea was full of creatures. And as Sedna sunk down, she was caught by all the creatures who had been born from her fingers. They carried their mother to a cave at the bottom of the sea. They decorated it with pearly shells and made a throne of coral. Sedna became Goddess of the Sea cared for by her children in her underwater palace. And the goddess sent her brothers fish, so that during the hard winter months they would never go hungry again. In gratitude they honoured the Goddess of the Sea.

Beneath the waves Sedna's black hair grew and grew. It spread out across the seabed, tangled and knotted. Sedna's hair scratched and pulled but she could not comb or plait it because she did not have fingers. She struggled and writhed, waves crashed on the shore and all the fish disappeared.
'The Sea Goddess is upset,' said Sedna's eldest brother. He paddled alone to the centre of the sea. A whirlpool carried him under the waves. He saw Sedna thrashing and moaning. She was caught in a forest of hair, entwined with shells, hooks, fishing nets, ropes, broken boats, all the flotsam and jetsam discarded by human beings. Tangled up in the rubbish were all the sea creatures. The eldest brother took a comb from his pocket and began to gently untangle Sedna's hair. He combed out all the rubbish and set loose the sea creatures. He combed out the knots until her hair was smooth. Then he plaited Sedna's hair into two, long thick ropes of braid that curled around the seabed. Sedna opened her arms with relief and sent her children back into the ocean.

Ever since then the people of the Arctic are careful not to forget the Goddess of the Sea. They visit Sedna once a year, to comb and plait her hair. They care for the great goddess so that the ocean is healthy and sea creatures thrive, that way Sedna, Goddess of the Sea, can care for us all.

There are several versions of this myth found across Alaska, Canada and Greenland where subsistence depends on living in harmony with nature. The myth is even more relevant today for the whole world. I have seen beautiful Inuit bone combs in collections at The British Museum, The Horniman Museum and The Pitt Rivers Museum. Some of these combs have a carved decoration on the top of a girl with very long plaits; myth merges with everyday practicality. In 2003 a small planet was discovered and named for Sedna, she sails across the universe now as well as under the sea.

Saule Shining One

Lithuania/Latvia

Saule Shining One who helps you on your journey? Who lights Saule's fire at dawn? It is her daughter Auzrine, bright Morning Star. Auzrine kindles a fire and wakes Saule. She feeds her mother creamy porridge and gets the horses ready. Saule puts on her ruby crown and climbs into a chariot of gold drawn by two diamond horses. She shakes the reins and the chariot sets off across the sky.

The chariot is a giant burning wheel. It rolls across the sky and Saule, Mother Sun, sows handfuls of gold and silver as she travels. They reach us down below and fill us with warm delight. Saule journeys all day until she reaches Paradise Island with its golden apple tree.

Saule tethers her horses, climbs the tree and lies along a branch. She picks a rosy apple and bites into its white flesh. Then her eyes begin to close. Saule Shining One who puts you to sleep? Who spreads Saule's bed at night? It is her daughter Wakarine, bright Evening Star. Wakarine feeds the horses, shakes out the downy quilt, plumps up the feather pillow and tucks her mother into bed. Wakarine sings a lullaby and kisses Saule goodnight. So the Shining One can continue her journey the next day and the next, our Mother Sun forever.

Primal Mother
of the Deep

Mesopotamia

When the world above and the world below were not yet named, there was nothing but water and air. A sea of salt and sweet waters, a sky of eternal darkness. Tiamat lived deep down in a watery abyss. Was the Primal Mother of the Deep, fish, serpent, hippo or great she-dragon? With vast mouth and swollen belly, scaly body and spiky tail, Tiamat, Begetter of All Things, slumbered. She dreamt, contemplating creation. When she was ready she whipped her tail in the water, her body rippled, scales swelled and broke open. Beings burst from her body – gods and goddesses of sky and earth, love and war, spring and storm were born.

There was nowhere for the gods and goddesses to go and nothing for them to rule. They sat on the dragon's back in the darkness listening to lapping water, waiting for light, waiting for earth. Who should be the ruler of this non-existent world? Who should be sovereign of all that might come? The gods and goddesses could not agree. Discussion turned to argument and their shouting disturbed Tiamat. The Primal Mother of the Deep was upset by her noisy offspring.

'Quiet!' she roared. 'Your argument is disrupting creation. Nothing can be born with this noise. I need to concentrate, to imagine. I need silence.' Tiamat whipped her tail, her body rippled, scales swelled and broke open. Beings burst from her body – demons and devils, scorpions with human heads, gigantic sharp-toothed snakes, towering centaurs, winged griffins with the heads of lions, slathering rabid dogs, serpents radiating lethal rays. The gods and goddesses ran for refuge along the dragon's back to the tip of Tiamat's tail. They stopped arguing and shivered with terror. And Tiamat returned to contemplation.

The God of Storms, Marduk, muttered, 'She who bore us is rejecting us. She who created us is destroying us. I will defeat Tiamat and kill her monstrous brood, on the condition I am king.'

The gods and goddesses agreed and Marduk armed himself for combat. He reached out into the darkness and caught four winds: Evil Wind; Tempest; Hurricane, and Whirlwind. He grasped them tight and pressed them beneath his arm, and with majestic strides marched along the dragon's spine towards her head.

Demons pressed around Marduk spitting and screeching. The Storm God lifted his arm and set Evil Wind free. It swirled through the demons tumbling them into the sea. Marduk cried, 'Mother of all, you are no mother of mine!'

Marduk loosed Tempest. It blew into Tiamat's mouth, pushing her lips apart. Tiamat writhed, her body a shuddering earthquake. Marduk set Hurricane free. It forced Tiamat's jaws open, filling her throat. The she-dragon began to pant. Marduk loosed Whirlwind. It howled down Tiamat's throat into her belly, filling it with air. The Primal Mother of the Deep could not breathe. Her jaws shook and she began to choke. Her belly expanded, her scaly skin stretching, her bones breaking, and her massive body burst in two.

The upper part of her body became the sky. The lower part of her body became the earth. The dragon's spine became mountain peaks, her soft belly the desert. Her breath became fog, her spit foam. Water ran from Tiamat's eyes and turned into two rivers. Two lovely rivers, the Tigris and the Euphrates. The rivers ran across dry sand turning the desert green. The Primal Mother of the Deep had become the world above and the world below. The great she-dragon is the Universe itself.

Marduk returned victorious.

'He went away a beloved son and returns a king!' cried the gods and goddess.

They crowned him ruler. Marduk surveyed earth with its two rivers and declared, 'I will build a city between these rivers. A city of great size and wealth, filled with dwellings and gardens. I will call it Babylon. In the centre I will build high Babel tower, a ziggurat to be the divine home of all gods and goddesses.'

And so mud bricks were fired and Babylon was built. In the centre a ziggurat of six levels rose up towards heaven, the Tower of Babel a landmark for all to see. The ziggurat was planted with flowers and trees, gardens that hung above the city. But the Primal Mother of the Deep could not stop crying, and is still crying. The Begetter of All weeps for the loss of her creative abyss. And her endless sweet and salty tears make the Tigris and the Euphrates flow.

This is my version of a much larger, more complex, creation myth, the Enuma Elish. It was written in cuneiform on stone tablets about 4000 BCE and is one of the oldest extant written texts. This myth was chanted, part of a performed ritual celebrating the New Year festival that was held in the spring. One of the things it describes is the end of a goddess, destroyed by a male god. The story continues on in the many dragon-slaying myths that appear throughout the world. I wanted to reclaim Tiamat as a generative source, which we can all visit!

Saraswati, Creator of Creation

India

A long time ago a river ran from high in the Himalayas all the way to the Gulf of Kutch. At her source she was sparkling and cold, refreshing the souls of all who drank or bathed. As the river flowed downstream she grew wide and stately, a place to gather with friends to spread out along her banks and rest. The river grew deeper and deeper and flowed out into the endless sea. The river is a goddess, Saraswati, she who makes life worth living. Her name means abundantly flowing. She is the flow of thought. Songs and poems bubble along her banks. Hers are waters of words, rivers of speech, oceans of stories.

Saraswati is the Goddess of Speech and Song, of creation itself. She sits on top of the highest mountain in the Himalayas wearing a pure white sari. She has four hands. In one hand she holds a book, in another a garland of flowers, in the third she holds a long-necked lute, the veena, with her fourth hand she strums its strings. Music fills the air, and streams of words and songs pour from her lips. It was Saraswati who invented the holy language of Sanskrit. And she who gave Soma, the nectar of immortality, to the gods.

The creator Brahma was so captivated by the Goddess Saraswati he gave himself a fifth head so that he could always see and hear her and she could never escape his gaze. Brahma's desire for Saraswati was so unnatural it disturbed the peace of the universe. Waves of lust circled earth, sun, moon and all the stars, unbalancing their positions in the heavens. Brahma's crazed passion was so violent it woke Shiva from his divine meditation. Shiva opened his third eye and turned into the God of Rage. He tore off Brahma's fifth head and the demented desire subsided. The sun, moon and stars returned to their proper courses and peace returned to the universe.

Saraswati knows that passion must be shaped in order to make art. And so she floats along her river on a swan. The swan glides graceful and serene. The surface of the river remains calm as a mirror and you cannot see the swan's feet paddling furiously beneath the water. Saraswati rides a white swan because she knows that creating art is hard work. She understands that all the effort of making art is invisible, hidden beneath the perfection of creation. Saraswati will hand you a pen, stop your notebook from blowing away, fill your pots with coloured inks, place a song and a story in your mind as light as down, make your feet tap and your fingers pluck. But before you pick up your paintbrush, put on your dancing shoes, or open your mouth, do not forget to ask, 'Goddess Saraswati may you reside on the tip of my tongue.'

The River Saraswati no longer runs to the sea. It disappears into a desert. This is said to be the result of a curse. May we protect all our rivers from such a fate. May our creative streams never run dry.

VIRGIN

Vesta Virgin Flame

Roman

Vesta tends the fires and keeps them burning. Is she a girl or a flame? Does she have fiery red hair hanging down her back? Or is she a glittering flame? Girl or flame – Vesta is radiantly beautiful and too hot to touch.

Vesta caught the eye of Mars, God of War, and he tried to woo her, but Vesta was not interested. Then Neptune God of the Sea asked for her hand in marriage. The gods laughed, what ill-advised coupling – the God of Water would extinguish his beloved immediately! Neptune insisted but Vesta's heart did not ignite. She went to Jupiter, father of the gods, and begged him, 'Allow me to remain unwed. Let me be forever virgin.'

Jupiter agreed and Vesta was filled with joy. She knelt by the fireplace and swept it clean. She placed a garland of flowers around the hearth, then lit a fire for Jupiter. 'I am burning desire satisfied by itself!' she declared. And filled his hearth and home with light and heat.

The fireplace became Vesta's altar and soon the goddess was worshipped in every house and temple with public and private fires. Loaves of bread, sheaves of wheat, millstones, donkeys all became sacred to Vesta. She became the patron of bakers. And was honoured at every wedding and funeral, for without

Vesta there is no party! Statues were carved of the goddess, some showing her holding a kettle or frying pan. Vesta chuckled, sparks flew, 'Tsss! Don't forget, I spit and bite!'

So Vesta was depicted as a burning phallus. Was she the fire-stick that brought fire into being? Or a blazing flame? Fire-stick or flame – Vesta became the Phallic Mother who kindles fire within herself.

One June, on the longest hottest night of the year, Cybele, Mother Earth, invited gods and spirits to a feast. Satyrs and nymphs arrived wrapped in garlands of flowers. Old Silenus rode his donkey laden with flasks of wine. Vesta wore a new robe of white wool. She rotated the fire-stick and kindled a fire from the setting sun – the feast could begin. Gods and spirits raised wine goblets to Cybele's bounty, then they drank, danced and sang until the early hours.

Vesta wandered off alone. She lay down in the long summer grass under the stars, closed her eyes and fell asleep. Her robe got caught up around her thighs, the fine cloth fell open at her neck, revealing a perfect breast. Priapus, the god who makes plants and male members grow, saw her. She looked so hot his phallus shot up. And it was unstoppable, it grew up and up stretching into the air. 'I will have her!' he mumbled.

He staggered towards Vesta, and old Silenus's donkey began to bray. 'Hee-haw! Hee-haw! Wake up! Wake up!'

Vesta was woken by her adoring follower. She burst into fiery flame, becoming a blazing phallus of fire that towered high above Priapus. His manhood shrank back, all his power shrivelled away. Priapus was surrounded by jeering gods and spirits. Outraged and accusing, they chased him into the dark woods. Vesta smoothed out her robe and wrapped her arms around the donkey.

'Thank you my noble friend. Your actions will never be forgotten.' And on the goddess's feast days, donkeys were garlanded with loaves of bread hung around their necks in gratitude for protecting Vesta.

Vesta's fire became so sacred it was kept alight night and day. It was believed that if her eternal flame was extinguished the City of Rome itself would be destroyed. Vesta's fire was tended by the Vestals, six virgins, chaste servants of the goddess. The girls wore robes of white wool, their feet bare, their hair loose. The Vestals swept the temple, decorated it with flowers and took turns to guard the flame and keep it alight. If the flame did go out, then the foolish girl who allowed it would be punished. Some said the punishment was whipping. Others said she would be buried alive in the Field of Wickedness and left to die in the cold ground. But once a year, at the start of spring, Vesta's flame was solemnly extinguished so that it could be renewed. The fire-stick was rotated and a new flame was kindled from the sun. Girl, flame, Phallic Mother – Vesta is alive again!

The beginning of March was when Vesta's flame was rekindled, but she had many other feast days throughout the year. Some Roman terracotta oil lamps are shaped liked phalluses, blessings for passionate nights perhaps, or honouring the Phallic Mother and her story!

Arianrhod

Wales

My castle appears at dawn, spinning crystal on the sea. My stronghold is a shining tower made of sea-light and stars. You can glimpse its pointed turrets at low tide far out in the bay. My fortress can be seen on a clear night, a circular crown in the heavens. This is the place poets come to for inspiration, to learn the wisdom of the cosmos. My castle revolves with the turning universe, with the rise and fall of the tides. It plays the music of the spheres, sings the song of sirens. Is it in the sea? Or is it in the sky? To reach my palace takes more than physical strength, more than navigation of waves or stars. If you do not have awareness, if you lack insight, then your journey will be wasted. Don't even bother setting out. You will fall to your death, drown, be ripped to shreds on the rocks before you reach my gate.

I am the virgin who gave birth. Twice. I stepped over the magic branch and my twins tumbled out. No one believed I was a virgin. Especially not Lord Math, who needed a virgin's lap to place his feet in to appease him from all the blood of wars and killings. Oh, the power of the virgin! I laughed with joy and surprise as my offspring appeared. My laughter turning to a shower of stars that no one could put out. Not even my own brother, Gwydion. It was he who had made me jump, and he stared in disgust, he was sure now that I had never been a virgin.

What had I been conceiving in my imagination? Unknown to me, to us all, the dark space within nurtures endless life. Oh, virgin power! That is the mystery all mothers and artists know, that something can be born from nothing. The first child to drop from my overflowing womb was beautiful wise Dylan ail Don. He leapt straight into the sea and swam away. Free flowing, rising, falling Dylan you never went away. My sea spirit I hear you turn tides, see you wash against the shore. The second child was fairest Lleu but I was not quick enough to catch hold of him and change his fate. That poor boy, what troubles, confusion, suffering was to be his and mine.

My brother caught the second child and carried him away. He put the boy in a chest with magic locks intending that this boy would be king. I tried to protect my child with spells. He would have no name. He would not bear arms. He would never marry a woman of this earth. He could only die in one rare situation. But a virgin giving birth was something Gwydion and Math could not conceive, it was an impossibility for them and together they set their course to destroy me.

They trapped and tricked me and one by one my spells were undone. Lleu's fate unravelled. Unknowingly I named my boy Lleu Llaw Gyffes. Later Lleu came to me in disguise. I did not recognise him and armed him to protect my castle against a fleet of war ships that vanished in the night as soon as I had given him a sword. Then Gwydion made a woman not of this earth. Blodeuwedd, Flower-Face, she smelled of summer flowers, oak, broom, meadowsweet and Lleu loved her. But maidens have their own desires and Gwydion could not control her. Blodeuwedd fell in love with another. And with her lover, Gronw, she constructed the one rare situation in which Lleu would meet his death.

But fair Lleu had magical origins, he knew charms and as the spear struck he turned into an eagle. Gwydion was filled with rage and used all his power to restore Lleu to human form and punish the lovers. He forced Gronw to die the death that was planned for Lleu. And turned Blodeuwedd into an owl with eyes like flowers. My brother got his wish, Lleu became king. He had made a king from deception, murder, trickery, just as all those in power are made.

I had not been able to guide the fate of my fair son. And ever since I have gathered lost souls. I collect the dead, soldiers fallen in battle, those who die fleeing terror. I collect them in my ship *Oar Wheel*. As it rolls across sea and stars, a whirling silver wheel, I ask Dylan for calm seas, I send Blodeuwedd to fly ahead and warn of danger. Then I guide the souls into new life. To all those who make it to my ship, to my castle I say live your own life, not mother, not wife, not even lover, only forever virgin.

This myth can be found in full in the Fourth Branch of the Mabinogi. Arianrhod's palace, Caer Arianrhod, is a rock formation off the coast of northern Gwynedd. It is sometimes visible at certain low tides and looks like turrets emerging from the sea. Caer Arianrhod is also used in Welsh as the name for the constellation Corona Borealis.

Changing Woman

*Navajo, Southwestern
United States of America*

Changing Woman is the law of existence. She changes young to old, moving to still, laughing to weeping and shows us how to change.

Changing Woman was born in a rain cloud on top of a mountain. Her mother was Darkness, her father Dawn. The baby girl lived on sunrays, pollen clouds and dew from flowers. First Woman and First Man came by, they were walking together in the mountains reuniting after an argument, a separation. They found the baby girl lying on a bed of flowers. They held her, hugged her close and took her home. The baby grew strong and as she grew she changed. She became a girl bathing in waterfalls, nourished by sunlight. Never remaining the same, the girl became a maiden.

One midsummer day it was so hot the maiden lay down in the bleached dry grass and fell asleep. She dreamt the Sun visited her in a blaze of golden light. The Sun embraced her, wrapping her in luminous heat, engulfing her. The girl woke up hot and sweaty. She looked about and saw that grasses were flattened, that bushes were blackened. She saw footprints burned into the dry ground, footprints disappearing into the west. It wasn't a dream. The Sun had visited her while she slept. The Sun had seduced her and she was no longer a maiden. She was changing.

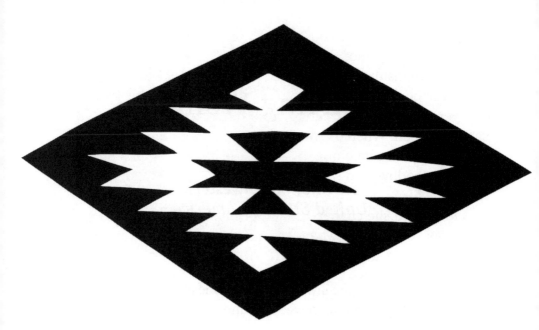

She felt warmth spreading across her belly, she was going to have a child. Her belly swelled and swelled. Until she gave birth, not to one child but to two, twins and boys. Never remaining the same, she changed again and became a mother.

The twins had been brought into the world with a purpose, to became warriors and slay monsters. When First Woman and First Man had separated, First Woman had satisfied her desire on her own. She found pliable sticks and juicy plants and enjoyed herself. From her deep pleasure monsters had been aroused. Her solo satisfaction had brought a race of demons into existence. The twins were destined to slay these monsters. But first they wanted to know who their father was.

Their mother sent them on a long journey to find the Sun. With the help of Grandmother Spider the twins met their father and killed the monsters. Except there were a few monsters that were so powerful they could not be killed: Old Age; Cold; Poverty; Hunger; Illness, and Death. These demons still exist and we suffer them all. When the twins returned to their mother she had changed. Never remaining the same, she had grown old. She bid her sons goodbye and set off on her own journey, walking west.

As she walked she changed again, becoming Changing Woman. She grew younger and younger until she had become a maiden and arrived on an island in the far Western Sea surrounded by four mountains. Changing Woman dances towards each mountain to bring us abundance. Dancing for rain in the east, for textiles in the south, for plants in the west, for animals in the north. And at the end of each day, as the sun sets in the western sky, she is visited by her lover and wrapped in luminous heat.

Changing Woman visits girls when they reach puberty. She stays with the maiden, living with her for a few days, dressing her in new clothes, singing songs, practising rites as the girl changes and becomes a woman. She blesses her with abundance and power. And reminds us all that change is inevitable and we should not be afraid. Changing Woman shows us how to change, to flow with change, grow with change, that change is beauty.

Changing Woman is an important and living Navajo goddess who also appears in other First Nations mythologies across the south and west of the United States. The myth of how the twins met their father is a long and symbolic quest for knowledge and some versions contain Grandmother Spider, who sits behind one of the boy's ears and whispers advice.

Being Bears for Artemis

Greece

The girls came to the shrine aged five or six. They were given short tunics to wear, took a vow to remain chaste and became bears for Artemis. They lived wild, learning to track and hunt, studying which plants healed and which harmed, running races with bare feet, learning how to fight and dance all in service to the Goddess Artemis. Her priestesses took the girls through the rites of passage from girlhood to womanhood. Sometimes the girls would put on saffron-coloured robes, dance with torches and make offerings to an altar beneath a date palm. Or they would dress as bears wearing masks and furs and become wild beasts. The girls became bears as offerings to the goddess to appease her and praise her. Being bears for Artemis brought food and fertility to everyone.

Artemis was the twin sister of Apollo. Their mother, the giantess Leto, had been raped by Zeus. Leto disguised herself as a wolf to escape the vengeance of Zeus's queen, Goddess Hera. With her belly swelling, the mother wolf made her way to the tiny island of Delos. The island was dry and desolate and there was no shady place where she could give birth. Leto laboured alone in the burning sun and gave birth to a girl, Artemis. As soon as she was born, Artemis sprang to her feet and helped her mother. She stood at Leto's head and feet simultaneously.

She became a date palm at her mother's head, giving her shade and sustenance. She crouched at her mother's heels, helping with the birth. She brought her twin brother Apollo into the light. And where she had knelt a fragrant feathery herb sprang up in the dusty soil; artemisia, a herb with potent healing powers. The twins had golden energy that radiated between them, mingling and merging so they were neither girl or boy but both. Artemis loved to hunt, Apollo to sing. Apollo became God of the Sun and Music. Artemis became Goddess of the Moon and Hunting.

Artemis carries a bow of gold, a quiver of silver arrows. When she runs the ground shakes, as she looses an arrow the forest moans and she leaves a trail of howling beasts behind her. Often Artemis hunts alone. Sometimes she is accompanied by her band of maidens, sworn virgins. They run with her until evening, then they find fresh water. Artemis hangs her bow from a tree and the maidens bathe the goddess, combing out her long hair, dressing her in fresh clothes. Then under the cool moon Artemis leads the girls in graceful dances.

Her favourite companion was Kallisto. She had vowed chastity like all of Artemis's maidens. One night when they were bathing in the moonlight, Artemis saw that her friend's belly was as round and swollen as the full moon. Artemis rose out of the pool in horror.

'You are with child? But you are under oath to renounce men!'

'It was not a man!' cried Kallisto. 'It was you! How could you forget our night of sweet passion? You came to me dressed as a bear. That is how I knew it was you!'

'It was not me,' said Artemis. 'I am not interested in sex, only in killing. It was that monster Zeus. He came to you in disguise. He did the same to my mother. Why didn't you resist? You broke your vow. You have betrayed me.'

'Please my Goddess, I adore only you.'

Artemis was filled with fury. She lifted her bow, aimed it at Kallisto and loosed a whistling arrow. It brushed Kallisto's shoulder and brown fur covered her body. Kallisto fell onto her hands and knees, and paws and claws appeared. Brown ears burst from her head and her swelling belly was covered with fur. Kallisto became a bear and she bounded away between the trees. Alone in the forest, the mother bear gave birth to a baby boy. Zeus flashed down, took the child, named him Arcus and gave him to the forest nymphs to raise. Then Zeus lifted the mother bear high above and placed her in the sky, a sparkling constellation, the Great Bear lumbering endlessly across the heavens showing us the way. When her son Arcus had reached the end of his life as King of Arcadia, he joined her in the sky as the Little Bear, the guiding Pole Star.

Artemis's vengeance was appeased and, lying in her pool with her maidens, she uttered a warning and pointed at the starry sky. Her maidens were chastened and would remain chaste. One day, seven of her virgins, sisters, stopped in a sunny glade to splash in a pool. When suddenly the giant Orion appeared. He was stalking deer and disturbed the maidens. The girls leapt out of the pool and fled. Orion was enflamed with lust and gave chase. The sisters were swift, trained by Artemis to run like gazelles, and Orion could not catch them. Orion pursued the seven sisters relentlessly for seven years. Artemis chased Orion, loosing arrow after arrow, but even she could not bring the giant down. Until the seven sisters were so exhausted their pace began to slow. Artemis pleaded with Zeus, 'I will never call you father but grant me a wish as a father should, save my girls.'

As Orion closed in on his prey there was a fluttering of wings and Zeus transformed the girls into a flock of doves. They beat their wings and flew up into the sky out of reach. Orion could not catch them. The sisters were so afraid they did not stop flying. They flew up into the heavens, where they became seven stars, seven doves, seven sisters, the Pleiades.

Artemis had lost her female companions. Enraged, she vowed to punish Orion. She hunted down a monstrous scorpion, trapped it and hid it on a track where the giant would pass. Orion trod on the beast and it stabbed him in the heel. Deadly poison rushed through Orion's body to his heart and he fell to the ground dead. Zeus lifted the giant up and set him in the heavens, a red star on his shoulder, a blue star on his heel, a whirling galaxy on the point of his sword. With dark wit, Zeus took up the deadly scorpion and placed that in the sky too. It became the constellation Scorpio and is still chasing Orion. But once a year the path of the moon passes close to the Pleiades and Artemis, Goddess of the Moon, can be with her virgin band again.

By becoming bears, girls honour Artemis. Crawling on hands and knees, dancing in furs and masks they become the one who will be killed. Being bears for Artemis draws the beast close, gives the hunter courage and promises a feast. In return the Goddess Artemis honours virgins with her protection, giving girls the sharpness of arrows and the strength of bows, so they may defend their precious maidenhood.

There are more myths of Artemis. And the story 'Diana Virgin Hunter' in this collection is a Roman version of the myth of Artemis and Actaeon.

Fair Maid of February

Ireland

Brigit, Brig, Bride was born with flames shooting out of her head like a bright crown. She was the daughter of the Daghda, chief of the Tuatha de Danann, the fairy people. As a baby she was fed on the milk of otherworld cows, which nourished her with healing powers. As a child she tended her father's fire, keeping it always alight.

As a young maiden she wove a white cloak and embroidered it with green leaves, buds, flowers. Every February Brigit puts on her cloak and radiant as a bride sweeps across the world. She spreads her cloak out over the earth and snowdrops appear. Brigit's fire warms the soil and the fair maids of February push their delicate white heads through the ground, snowdrops arrive, herald to the spring.

'In with the fire, out with the frost!' Brigit cries.

She stokes her fire, earth grows warm, the sun returns and the days grow longer. Cailleach groans. The crone carries the frost, Cailleach brings cold winds wherever she goes and wants winter to last as long as possible.

'Let Bride in,' cries Brigit. 'Let her come!'

Cailleach is forced to lose her cold grip and put her icy staff down beneath a holly bush.

'The bride of the feast is here! Spring has come!' cries Brigit.

As her cloak swirls over the world it leaves behind fresh dew. The dew sparkles in the spring sunshine. People go out at dawn to gather the dew in cupped hands, rags and saucers. They bathe their eyes, drink the dew, rub it on their faces. The dew is holy, healing, it makes you beautiful. Brigit hangs her cloak up on a sunbeam to dry, then puts it away for another year. Goddess Brigit is the patron of poets, smiths and midwives. She brings the flash of inspiration, the flame of creativity, the spark of life. Brigit blesses the germination of seeds, the flowing of milk in animals and the running of water in springs.

Brigid, Brig, Bride was born with a face like a flower. She was the daughter of a farmer. She took care of the cows and sheep, milking the animals, making butter and cheese. When anyone passed the farmyard Brigid would offer them churns of fresh milk, pats of butter and creamy cheese. Her father was not pleased but was unable to stop her. Brigid loaded a cart up with food and went out to feed the poor. The more she gave away, the more milk the animals produced and the more beautiful Brigid became. So her father arranged for his daughter to marry. But Brigid refused, she wanted to remain a virgin. The only bride she would be was a bride of Christ. One suitor sneered at her choice never to marry, Brigid glanced at him and his eye exploded. Another suitor looked her up and down lasciviously and she plucked out her own eye and threw it on the ground to repulse him.

Brigid would be a virgin and a bride. She clothed herself in robes of white and founded the first convent under a grove of oak trees in Kildare. Other maidens joined her and together they prayed and sang and took care of the poor. The sisters always kept a fire burning, night and day, a flame for the new light that had come. Brigid's perpetual fire burned for a thousand years until it was extinguished in the reformation when places of worship, convents and monasteries were destroyed.

On the first of February when the snowdrops peep through the ground, light a candle and place the burning flame in the soil to warm the earth. Greet Brigit, Brigid and ask her to bless you with heat and light. Weave a cross from grass with four arms of equal length, one for each of the seasons. Hang the cross over your door and welcome in the Fair Maid of February.

Brigit is both pagan goddess and Christian saint and her two stories contain echoes of each other. Her feast day, 1 February, is an ancient pagan festival and a saint's day. There are many stories of healing and miracles linked to Saint Brigid. There is also a sweet story about how she was a midwife to the Virgin Mary and distracted King Herod's soldiers by wearing a mesmerising crown of candles on her head! This story seems to bring the aspects of goddess and saint together, and is reminiscent of Swedish Saint Lucia, who also wears a crown of candles.

Idunn's Apples

Scandinavia

Idunn, the Rejuvenating One, was always young. Barely a maiden, Idunn had skin as plump as a teenager's and forever fresh eyes that looked at the world as if she had never seen it before. She was eternally virgin, yet Idunn was mother to all the gods. She had a casket filled with golden apples. She carried the casket wherever she went and only she could open it because its treasure was priceless. The casket contained eternal youth, the apples of immortality. Idunn only opened her casket for the gods, feeding them apples so all illness disappeared, wounds healed, ageing vanished and the gods became young and strong. Idunn could never give away all her apples because her casket was always full. The maiden gave birth to the gods again and again and again. And the gods adored her.

Idunn laughed, 'The secret to eternal youth is not my apples.'

She clasped poet Bragi's hand and led him to their hall. Their home was always filled with laughter, golden joy shone from the doors and windows, there was always food and wine, poems and stories. And everyone wanted to be with them.

Idunn's apples were known throughout the nine worlds, and the dwarfs and giants wanted immortal life too. Loki, Trickster God, offered to get the apples for the giants in exchange for an old debt, the debt of his life. The giant Thiazi agreed and Loki ran to Idunn's hall.

'Rejuvenating One, you will not believe what I have seen!' Idunn was giggling, lying in Bragi's lap as he told her a story.

'Nothing can be as extraordinary as this tale!' she said. 'Sit with us Loki, listen!'

'There is no time!' said Loki. 'You must come. A tree has appeared on the edge of the forest covered in golden apples. They look just like yours, but perhaps a little bigger.'

Idunn sat up, 'Bigger! That is impossible. And there are no other apples like mine.'

She picked up her casket and kissed Bragi. 'Your story must wait, I have to see these apples. Lead me.'

Loki led Idunn out of Asgard, the palace of gods, over Bifrost, the flaming rainbow bridge to the edge of the forest. Idunn looked about, 'Where is this tree?'

Suddenly the sky grew dark and there was the whirring of wings. A giant eagle swooped down, caught Idunn in his claws and soared into the air. The maiden's screams echoed through the trees and Loki looked away. He felt a pang of guilt, but not for long; he'd saved his own life.

The eagle carried Idunn to the high mountains of Jotunheim, the land of the giants, to a stone tower perched on a sheer cliff. The eagle swooped through a doorway, dropped Idunn to the ground and turned into Thiazi, glowering Giant of Storms.

'Give me an apple so I may be a god.'

Idunn held out her casket, 'Take one.'

Thiazi grabbed the golden box and could not open the lid. He forced his huge fingers against the lock, used all his might, but it would not move. 'Open it!' he roared.

'Never!' said Idunn.

'You'll change your mind!'

The giant dragged Idunn to a chamber of jagged rocks. An icy wind howled through gaps in the stones. Idunn sat down, pulled her thin cloak around her shoulders, hugged her casket and tried to remember one of Bragi's poems.

The gods began to feel stiff, their bones ached and skin wrinkled, their hair turned white and teeth fell out. The gods grew old. Even Odin, the most powerful, hobbled around on a stick, his back bent, eyes dim and mind no longer sharp. Odin gathered the gods. All were present except Idunn and Loki. The trickster was found lying on his bed withered and grey, and brought before Odin.

'Fetch Idunn,' ordered Odin. 'Bring her back or you will meet your death.'

'Death if I do, death if I don't,' muttered Loki. 'I will need Freyja's falcon suit.'

Freyja, Goddess of Sex, just as magnificent in old age, held out her suit of feathers. 'Take care of it,' she said. 'Bring back youth.'

Loki pulled on the magical feathers and turned into a falcon. He flew to Jotunheim, peered through a gap in the stones and saw Idunn sitting alone shivering, her arms wrapped around her casket. Loki swiftly touched stones with wings and a gap appeared. The falcon flew through, into the chamber, touched Idunn and turned her into a small brown nut. He caught her in his claws and flew back to Asgard.

When the Storm Giant found his captive missing, he gave chase. The giant eagle pursued the falcon. The eagle's great wings beat up a storm, buffeting the falcon. Odin saw the two birds and cried, 'Heap wood around the walls of Asgard!'

The ancient gods struggled to pile branches, chairs, barrels along the walls. As the birds approached, Odin gave a signal and the gods set light to the wood. The wood smouldered and the falcon flew over the walls of Asgard. As the giant eagle followed the wood burst into flame and the Storm Giant was consumed by fire.

Loki threw off his falcon suit, opened his fist and dropped the nut to the ground. Idunn appeared holding her golden casket, young and fresh as an apple. She looked at the elderly gods, 'You may eat, but you must protect me and my apples forever more.'

The gods vowed, bit into the golden flesh and grew young again. Bragi took Idunn's hand, and she laughed, 'The secret to eternal youth is not my apples.' She kissed Bragi. 'Finish your story!'

And they went back to their hall, to the golden light of poems and the eternal spirit of stories.

Apples and nuts were sacred food for the people of Scandinavia, symbols of eternal life and fertility. They were carved onto grave stones, decorated shields and woven into textiles. And both apples and nuts were placed inside graves.

Morning Star,
Evening Star

Lithuania/Latvia

Auzrine was not always Morning Star, Wakarine was not always
Evening Star. The two maidens lived with Saule, Mother Sun.
The girls did not know who their father was. Their mother had
three husbands, Sky, Moon and Storm. Different husbands for
different moods. Saule loved Sky at midday when she was at
her peak, her zenith. She loved Moon when she was setting and
it was getting dark. And she loved Storm when she was hot and
fiery. Auzrine and Wakarine did not know which one was their
father, and so they had three fathers.

The fathers were not around much. They appeared when Saule
wanted them. And she sent them away as soon as she had enjoyed
them. Sky took up too much space. Moon was not faithful. He
was a charmer, always having affairs. And Storm could not help
spoiling Saule's laundry! His thunderstorms ruined her fresh
sheets and pillow cases, her white shirts and yellow ribbons. So
Saule did not spend much time with her husbands. Instead, her
daughters helped her to rise and set and fill the world with light.

On the first day of spring, Saule rose earlier than usual. Auzrine dressed her mother quickly and hitched up the diamond horses. Then Saule set off to herald spring and warm the world. Moon was still shining and he watched Saule's fiery chariot roll away across the sky. Moon peeped through his wife's windows and spied Auzrine moving around the kitchen, washing up the porridge pot and putting it away. She had become such a bright maiden! Moon was filled with desire. He slipped through the house and caught Auzrine around the waist, filling her face with silver light. He seized Auzrine tight and she cried out in fear. But Moon did not stop, he steered the maiden to Saule's bed, threw her down and pressed his huge round body over hers. He covered Auzrine with his shining weight so she could not move. Then Moon violated his own daughter and Auzrine howled in horror.

Storm heard her cries and dashed to help. Storm battered Moon, pounding Moon with wind and rain, thrashing him with hail and ice. Auzrine huddled in a corner while Storm raged. At last Storm abated. The house was flooded with water and Moon had gone.

Wakarine waded through the water to save her sister, and floating in the water she found pieces of silver. Moon had been torn to bits! Wakarine cried out in rage. Moon might be a monster but he was still her father. She gathered up all the broken pieces of silver. She spread them out to dry, then tried to put her father back together. But she could not make the pieces match or fit. Wakarine could not mend Moon, she could not make her father whole again.

When Saule returned she found both her daughters weeping. And she wept too, red tears that fell like berries covering Earth.

'I will never share my house with Moon!' cried Saule. 'I will not even share the sky with Moon. I never want to see his face.'

Saule banished Moon to the night sky so they would never meet again. Wakarine could not put Moon back together and Moon is still in pieces, and has been waxing and waning ever since. And you can still see the deep grey scars from Storm's battle marking Moon's face. But Wakarine could not forsake her father. So Wakarine became Evening Star, shining as Moon rises, guiding her father across the dark sky. Auzrine stayed with her mother and became Morning Star, shining as the sun rises, guiding her mother across the sky into light.

Goddess of the Hunt

Roman

Diana is the virgin Goddess of the Woods. She is Guardian of Wild Beasts, Protector of Animals and also Goddess of the Hunt. She loves what is untamed and is herself untameable. Her joy is to run across hills and mountains. Her sport is chasing wild creatures. But all the animals she hunts take shelter under her.

Diana's father was the great god Jupiter, her mother is unknown. She could have been an underworld Titan, a sea-nymph, a spirit of plenty or countless others seduced by Jove. Whoever she was, she instilled in Diana determination to escape and to never submit. When Diana was still a young child her father lifted her onto his knee and said, 'What gift can I give my little maid?'

Diana replied, 'I want a bow, Father and a quiver full of sharp arrows. I want a tunic that only reaches to my knees so that I may run freely. And I want a band of maidens to run with me and keep me company. But most of all, give me my virginity, Father. Give me my maidenhood to keep forever.'

Then she reached up and tugged Jupiter's beard, something a woman might do to tease her husband. Jupiter laughed and said, 'You may have it all my child,' and bowed his head to confirm his words.

He set Vulcan to work at once. The Blacksmith God pumped up the fires in his forge and hammered out a bow of shining silver shaped like the crescent moon. He forged a quiver of sharp arrows. A short tunic was woven. Diana pulled it on, tied a belt around her waist and caught her hair up into a knot. Then she took the quiver on her back, hung the bow from her shoulder and strode off into the forest alone.

Diana made her home in the leafy woods. Her legs and arms turned golden from the sun. Her left shoulder bore the quiver strap and became muscular. And when she used her bow she would loose her tunic and bare her right breast so she could hold the bow firmly against her chest. Young girls followed the Goddess of the Hunt, racing after her.

'If you want to be my companions – you must swear,' said Diana. And she made each maiden place a hand upon her bow and promise, 'This bow is witness to my virginity. I will keep my maidenhood forever.'

The maidens ran with the Goddess of the Woods through groves and gorges, along wild mountain paths. They accompanied Diana as she tracked and chased deer, lynx, stag. They studied the Goddess of the Hunt as she loosed arrows, slaying hare, boar, bear. When she was tired of hunting Diana would search for a watery glade. The maids would place Diana's sacred weapons against the trees and decorate the branches with garlands of flowers in gratitude for all the prey the goddess had killed. Then the maidens would lift Diana's tunic over her head, untie her hair and lead her to the water. They would wash away the blood and dirt of the hunt. And Diana would take onto her lap the baby animals she had saved and let them suckle from her breast. She would not forget to leave food and water at the edge of the forest for the wild beasts. So they would willingly come the next day and sacrifice themselves to her. Torches would be lit and Diana and her maidens would feast and dance until dawn. Goddess Diana was both predator and protector.

One hot day Actaeon was out hunting. He had learned the art of hunting from Chiron the centaur, half-man half-horse. Actaeon spent his time following his beloved dogs through the pathless woods hunting with nets and spears. Actaeon came upon some trees hung with flowers, he ordered his dogs to sit and walked into the grove. He heard water splashing and saw a woman bathing. She was surrounded by maidens, laughing and showering her with water. Actaeon stared in wonder as water trickled down the woman's neck, trailing along her golden limbs and bare breasts. Diana looked up and saw the hunter standing still and staring as if in a spell. The maidens screamed and Diana reached for her bow, but her weapons lay under the trees. She swiftly cupped her hand in the pool and sent a streak of water flashing through the air like an arrow. Sharp water struck Actaeon's face. He flinched, water ran down his brow and his cheek smarted. Diana cried, 'You are nothing but a beast. And you will never speak of what you have seen.'

Actaeon's head began to itch, furry horns pushed up from beneath his wet hair and grew into a crown of antlers. His neck thickened and arms stiffened. Actaeon fell onto all fours and his hands and feet hardened into hooves. Thick red-brown fur covered his body. Actaeon opened his mouth to cry and uttered a low grunt. Actaeon twitched his tail, stamped his hooves and bolted, bounding away between the trees.

The Goddess of the Hunt leapt out of the water and turned into a doe. She chased the stag, driving him towards his own dogs. Actaeon's tracker dog, Blackfoot, had been trained well and knew the scent of stag. Blackfoot gave chase, and sharp-nosed Mountain Ranger and swift Gazelle followed close behind. River with muscles rippling, and Whirlwind the powerful bounded over rocks and stones with ears pricked. Wingdog raced ahead. Sheen with snow-white coat caught the scent and ran swiftly. Spartan wiry and tough, Wolfcub, and Whitefang chased over crags. Diana urged the stag towards the pack. Pursuer was now the pursued. The pack surrounded the stag, gnashing and drooling. Actaeon was afraid of his own dogs, the pack he loved, who had served him so faithfully. He wanted to shout, 'Stop my hounds, it is I, your master, the one who feeds you, the one who cares for you.'

But the words would not come, all the stag could do was bellow. The dogs were swift and the pack split, circling the prey. Montaignard, Morpelu and Dyamond were the strongest and the dogs Actaeon loved the most, they pinned their master to the ground just as they had been taught.

Then the whole pack fell on Actaeon, burying their fangs into his body. Diana watched as Actaeon was torn to pieces by his own hounds. And only when Actaeon was dead, did the Goddess of Hunting cool her anger and return to her maidens.

The dogs sat by the kill, panting and waiting for their master to praise and pat them for their skill. But their master did not come. The dogs howled. Then ran through the forest to Chiron's cave, thinking their master would be there. The Centaur understood and followed the whimpering hounds back to the bloodied mess spreading across the forest floor. Chiron carved an image of Actaeon from wood to soothe the dogs' grief. And the pack lay around it, but the image never reached out to stroke or feed them and in the end they forgot Actaeon and found a new master.

Woe betide those who pursue Diana, pursue any virgin when she does not choose to be pursued. Woe betide those who compete with the Goddess of the Hunt in shooting stags. Woe betide those who do not take care of the woods. And woe betide those who forget Diana's yearly dance, those who do not perform her holy rites. So clean up the forest paths. Let weeds and mushrooms flourish in the woods. Decorate trees with garlands of flowers. Worship a cut apple bough. Call a branch the goddess. Then holding shields and wearing short tunics let your quivers rattle and dance in a circle, beating your feet loudly and singing, 'Hail Goddess of the Wood, Great Goddess of the Tunic, Diana Virgin Hunter, protect us now.'

Diana is the Roman version of Artemis and absorbed much of her mythology. But for me she is a distinct goddess in her own right who has been depicted over and over again in myriad forms of art across the centuries.

Maiden, Mother of All

Christian

Queen of Virgins, Star of the Sea, Mystical Rose, Mother Most Merciful, Gate of Heaven, Morning Star, Our Lady, Holy Mary.

Mary went to the well to fetch water and a bright light shone around her. She heard a voice, 'Hail Mary, full of grace, the Lord is with you.'

Mary looked about but could not see anyone. She filled her jug with water and the light gathered, grew and took the form of an angel with brilliant wings. Mary was terrified and hid her face. The angel said, 'Be not afraid. You have been chosen above all women to bear the incarnate Son of God. All generations will call you blessed. Your name will be magnified across the earth.'

Mary stood trembling and bewildered, 'How shall I bear a child when I am a virgin? I am unmarried and know not a man!'

'Fear not Mary,' said the angel, 'the Holy Spirit will protect you, the power of the Most High will support you. You are to be Maiden, Mother of All, and you will conceive his word.'

A ray of golden light shone on Mary's head. The light illuminated Mary's face and she was flooded with love. A beam of light entered Mary's ear. And she conceived the word through her ear. Mary conceived the word in heart and mind. A child would be born! Mary was filled with light and joy and cried, 'Behold! The handmaid of the Lord.'

Mary had been dedicated as a temple virgin when she was a little girl. She had skipped up the steep temple steps by herself. At the top of the steps the High Priest and elders were waiting and they bid the little girl sit down and rest after her great climb. But Mary pointed her toe and began to dance! Her tiny feet expressed her joy. She twirled and whirled, and wonder seized all who watched her dancing. The High Priest said, 'Sometimes the spirit can only be expressed through dancing.'

With the other temple virgins, Mary learned to read and sew. One day she was sewing a white cloth and she pricked her finger. Seven drops of blood fell onto the linen, and as Mary looked at the blood shivers of joy and shivers of sorrow passed through her, and she did not understand why. Later, along with the other maidens, she sewed a long gossamer veil for the temple. It was a delicate curtain made of silk shot through with purple, gold and scarlet threads. The veil took many months to make. When it was ready it was hung from ceiling to floor and shimmered in the breeze. The High Priest said, 'Sometimes the spirit can only be expressed through sewing.'

The veil would hang in the temple for more than thirty years. Until the moment that Mary's son, Jesus, was crucified, then the veil would split in two, from ceiling to floor, and no one would understand how.

When the temple virgins reached puberty, the High Priest arranged their marriages, but Mary refused to marry. The Priest prayed for guidance and an angel appeared, saying, 'Gather the unmarried and widowed men, tell each to bring a staff. The Lord will choose Mary's husband.'

Men arrived at the temple, each carrying a staff. Among them was Joseph, a carpenter, his back hunched from hard work, his hair and beard white. His wife had died some years before and he was lonely. He was not carrying a staff, just an old plank of wood from his workshop. Each man stepped forward and placed their staff on the altar, hoping they would be chosen. But nothing happened, there was no angel, no sign from God and each man stepped back again. Then it was Joseph's turn.

The other men chuckled, 'He couldn't even bring a proper staff. If we weren't chosen, he won't be!'

Joseph placed his plank on the altar. Green shoots began to uncurl from the old wood, buds broke through and the dry plank burst into white blossom. The temple was filled with the scent of spring.

The Priest said, 'This is the sign of the Lord. Joseph is to be betrothed to Mary.'

Joseph was suddenly afraid, 'She is a maid and I am an old man. It is not fitting.'

But the High Priest insisted, 'The Lord God has chosen.'

Joseph courted Mary, and one day they walked together through an orchard. They passed a cherry tree filled with ripe fruit. The cherries smelled so sweet, Mary reached into the tree to pick some fruit, but the branches were too high. 'Joseph, pluck me a cherry,' she said. 'I am filled with such longing for a cherry, it must be because I'm with child.'

'We are not yet married!' cried Joseph. 'How can you be with child? We do not know each other as man and wife and you have betrayed me already. Let the one who stole your cherry pick you cherries!'

'I am a virgin,' said Mary. 'And this child is the Son of God.'

She told Joseph of the angel's message. But Joseph shook his head, 'I was a fool to become engaged to one so young. And I have been made a fool of.'

Then a tiny voice spoke, 'Bow down, cherry tree!'

A little voice spoke from Mary's womb, 'Bow down, cherry tree, bow down low, so my gentle Mother may eat your fruit. Bow down so my Virgin Mother may eat your sweet fruit.'

The cherry tree began to shiver, the branches shook and the top most branches of the tree bent low to the ground. Mary picked a handful of cherries and popped them into her mouth. Joseph was astonished and knelt before Mary,

'Forgive me,' he said. 'I am the fool. An old fool who is honoured to be the father of the Son of God.'

After their wedding, Joseph and Mary travelled to Bethlehem as all citizens were commanded to return to their birthplace and pay taxes. The town was crammed with people and they could not find a place to stay. Night fell and Mary suddenly felt the child coming. On the edge of town they found a tumbledown stable, it would have to do. And Joseph left Mary in her birth pangs and went to find a midwife.

As he walked back into town, the wind suddenly hung still, the river stopped rushing, all the dogs fell silent. Joseph passed an inn and people sat poised, food and drink held to their mouths, their fingers pointing upwards. Everyone was looking up at the sky, at a brilliant star. Then suddenly the wind blew and they all began eating and talking again.

Joseph found two experienced midwives, Hepzibah and Salome. But when they arrived at the stable it was shrouded in a thick cloud, wrapped in darkness and they were unable to enter. At last the cloud lifted and the stable was filled with light. The same bright star was shining down on the humble dwelling and Mary was holding a baby wrapped in her veil. Hepzibah, the older midwife, lifted Mary's robes to examine the new mother and make sure the birth was finished.

'Oh my!' cried Hepzibah. 'This girl is still a virgin!'

'That's impossible!' said Salome, the younger midwife. 'Look! There is a baby! Have you been drinking tonight? Or perhaps you're getting too old for this job.'

Hepzibah shook her head, 'If you don't believe me sister, see for yourself.'

Salome examined Mary and cried, 'It's true! And a miracle! This girl is a virgin!'

But as Salome removed her hand it began to wither, her fingers twisted and knotted into a claw. Salome could no longer move her hand, it was paralysed.

Salome wept, 'I did not believe and now I have lost my hand. Forgive me Holy Virgin, restore my hand so I may help all mothers.'

The newborn baby spoke, 'Touch me, touch me.'

Salome reached out and touched the baby's soft cheek. Her hand was filled with warmth and life. Movement returned to her hand and Salome bowed, 'Great Lady I will serve you to the end of my life.'

Mary rocked the baby, and Joseph and the midwives watched in wonder. Until their eyes felt heavy, their heads began to nod and they fell into a sleep filled with dreams. Mary whispered, 'Tell me darling son, what is your destiny?'

The baby spoke, 'My dear Mother those seven drops of blood you saw are the seven joys and seven sorrows that you will suffer because of me. Joy at my birth and sorrow at my death. You will watch me die and be buried beneath a stone. You and the world will weep for me. Then you will see me rise again, like the sun and the moon that always return, so life will return for me. And you and the world will rejoice for me. Then you will be crowned Queen of Heaven. And you will be called Queen of Virgins, Star of the Sea, Mystical Rose, Mother Most Merciful, Gate of Heaven, Morning Star, Our Lady, Holy Mary. Maiden, Mother of All.'

There are many more legends, folktales, carols, apocryphal stories, frescos and paintings about the Virgin Mary, many linked to miracles. This particular story has been made by mixing together bits of: the Bible; The Golden Legend; Medieval Mystery plays; folktales and carols popular in medieval times across Europe. The Virgin Mary has many feast days along with additional local feast days all over the world. The day that the angel visited Mary is celebrated as the Annunciation on 25 March.

WARRIOR

Battle of Day and Night

Sumeria

In the first days, in the very first days, in the first nights, in the very first nights a tree grew, a huluppu tree. The tree was nurtured by the waters of the Euphrates and a warm wind blew through its branches. The tree flourished, its branches grew wide, its trunk strong.

Innana, Queen of Day, passed by. 'What a beautiful tree,' she said. 'This tree belongs to me! It will make a holy throne to sit upon, a golden bed to lie on.' Innana tended the tree. She settled the earth around the tree with her foot, and poured water on the roots.

Lilith, Queen of Night, passed by. 'What a beautiful tree,' she said. 'This tree belongs to me! It will make a holy throne to sit upon, a golden bed to lie on.' Lilith climbed into the tree and stretched herself along a branch. 'This tree will be my home.'

The stately Anzu bird flew down and made its nest at the top of the tree. The serpent that cannot be charmed coiled itself around the roots. The tree grew thick, its bark did not split. Joy filled Lilith and she sang, rejoicing in her home.

Years passed and Innana asked, 'How long must I wait until I have a shining throne? How long until I have a shining bed? It must be time.'

Innana hung a sword from her side and went to cut down her tree. But she found a serpent gnawing at the roots, and a bird sitting in a nest at the top of the tree feeding its young. And lying along a branch, she found a maiden, eating an apple.

'This tree is my throne,' cried Innana.

'This tree is my home,' replied Lilith.

'I watered it. I cared for it!' said Innana.

'And I live in it!' said Lilith.

They could not agree who owned the tree. Innana wept, but the maid, the bird and the snake would not leave the tree.

Innana went to her eldest brother Utu and begged for his help. Utu refused. Inanna's younger brother, the warrior Gilgamesh, heard his sister weeping. He lifted his bronze axe to his shoulder and marched to the tree. He took the trunk in his massive hands and shook the tree. Lilith clung to the branches. The Anzu bird and its young flew from the tree top. Gilgamesh struck the snake with his axe and split the serpent that cannot be charmed in two. Lilith screamed. But Gilgamesh loosened the soil and pulled up the tree. He pulled the roots right out of the ground and tore up Lilith's home. Then Gilgamesh lifted the tree onto his shoulders and carried it back to Innana's palace. At last she had a golden throne to sit upon, a golden bed to lie on.

Lilith had been forced from her home. She roared with rage. She opened her arms and two black wings appeared and curled claws burst from her feet. Lilith flapped her dark wings, flew up into the air and soared to the uninhabited places. Lilith lived alone in the wild places, surrounded by her companions, owls, snakes, lions. And there the Queen of Night planned her revenge.

This story is the oldest version of the myth of the woman, tree, snake and bird. It was written down in cuneiform on stone tablets in Ancient Mesopotamia over 4,000 years ago. Sumerian cylinder seals repeatedly show the elements of goddess, tree, horned god and serpent. The motifs in this story were widespread and very important. This story grew, put down roots, sent up shoots, scattered seeds and tales sprang up across different countries, languages, religions and cultures. You can find one version of what happens next at the end of this chapter!

Pele, Volcano Goddess

Hawaii

I am the earth eater, the land maker. I dispel darkness with red-hot flame. I burn paths, forge new land. I transform from inside out. My fire is righteous, my lava purifying. My word is final.

Pele left her family in a cloud of smoke. She could no longer live with them, she set fire to everything. Her mother gave her a pearl-like egg. 'Care for this egg until it hatches. It will become your sister and she will help you.'

Pele tucked the egg between her breasts and climbed into a carved canoe. She paddled for months looking for a home. Island after island she stopped and dug pits deep enough to hold her fire. Her siblings raced after her, flooding the pits with water, filling them with rocks, extinguishing her flame. Until Pele came to Hawai'i. On the summit of Mount Kīlauea she dug a vast fire pit and filled it with sulphurous gases, bubbling lava, spitting flames. She created a volcano so deep, so hot, no one could put it out. And there, Pele Volcano Goddess made her home.

I am fiery desire. Sizzling, licking flames. My fire is seductive, my heat all embracing.

Pele took the form of a woman, a ravishing beauty with lava black hair and burning eyes. She took the Great Boar,

Kamapua'a, as a lover. He was a tall warrior but along his back were the rough bristles of a hog. He spent his time digging the earth with a pig's snout, churning up muck with boar's trotters. Kamapua'a dug up so much mud he began to extinguish Pele's fire. The Volcano Goddess spewed out blistering words, 'We can never be together!'

So they agreed to live on opposite sides of the island. Pele took the leeward side where it is dry and hot. Kamapua'a took the windward side where it is windy and rainy. And so the two climates of Hawai'i came into existence.

The pearly egg hatched and Pele's sister, Hi'iaka, was born. She was loyal and took care of Pele. Especially when Pele lay down on her bed of red-hot coals. Then her body would change, it would become dry, wrinkled, old. Pele turned into an old woman and would sleep for nine days and eight nights while her spirit wandered. Hi'iaka kept guard, watching over her sister until the nine days and eight nights had passed, and then she would sing her sister's spirit back into her body.

One time, Pele's spirit left her body and took the form of a radiant woman with lava black hair. Pele's spirit heard the sound of singing and dancing and followed the sound to the far side of the island. There she saw Lohiau, a young man, dancing freely. He beckoned to the shining beauty. Pele danced with him, teasing, seducing, igniting a fire inside Lohiau that was so hot he was enraptured. Nine days and eight nights passed, and Hi'iaka began to sing. 'Wake, wake Goddess. Awake my sister. Lift up your head, Bright Lightening Shaft. Rise up, Blazing Eyes of Heaven. Return, Flame of my Heart.'

Pele felt a longing for her fire mountain, she needed to go home to her bed of flames. 'I will return,' she said to Lohiau. He watched Pele flicker, fade and vanish and felt his heart would break.

I am the heat of love, the burning heart. I am all-consuming infatuation that will destroy itself.

Pele opened her eyes, 'I'm in love, dear sister,' she said. 'I beg you bring Lohiau here. I cannot leave my mountain again.'

Hi'iaka sighed, 'It is such a long journey.'

'If you bring him we can share him,' said Pele. 'I will have him for the first five days, then we can share him after that.'

Hi'iaka agreed. She put on her magic skirt and set off. She drove back fog and mist by swishing her skirt. She stopped freezing wind and piercing rain sweeping the hem of her magic skirt. When the sun came out she saw the majesty and beauty of the island, and songs, poems, chants poured from her lips filling the island and they still remain today.

On a lonely cliff she found Lohiau. He was lying on a funeral bier covered with flowers. He could not live without Pele and had starved himself to death. Hi'iaka began to chant, calling up his spirit. She sang his spirit back into his body. His spirit returned through his eyes into his chest, through his limbs into his loins and Lohiau sat up.

Hi'iaka led him back to Pele. On the long journey she swirled her skirt to protect them both, and they shared songs and stories. By the time they arrived on Pele's fiery mountain, Lohiau had fallen in love with Hi'iaka, the sister who had resurrected him.

I am smouldering anger. A volcano of unstoppable wrath. My raging flames burn everything in their path.

Hi'iaka placed a garland of flowers around Lohiau's neck to welcome him home. Pele watched as her sister stood close to Lohiau and greeted him nose to nose. Pele saw Lohiau clasping her sister, hugging Hi'iaka tight, pulling her towards him.

Flames of fury flickered around Pele's feet as she watched her sister and her lover sink to the ground in a passionate embrace. They rolled their bodies on top of each other, pressed themselves together unable to resist for a moment longer. Pele burst into flames.

'The first five days were mine!' Boiling lava erupted. 'My word is final!'

Molten lava poured across the ground. Hi'iaka and Lohiau ran and Pele raced after them, raging fire poured from her mouth, streams of lava flowed from her hair. They could not run fast enough. Red-hot lava engulfed Lohiau, turning him into a pillar of hard, black rock. His second life had ended.

Hi'iaka swirled her skirt, journeyed to the land of the dead and sang Lohiau out of the underworld. When Pele saw that life had returned to Lohiau a third time, she said, 'I loved you in a different life, that time has gone.' She picked up a white sea shell and gave it to her sister. Hi'iaka placed it on the waves and it turned into a boat. Hi'iaka and Lohiau climbed into the white boat and sailed away, leaving the Volcano Goddess alone, blazing with light on top of her mountain.

My fire will never go out. I burn without end. My flames smoulder in the deepest place. I boil over, erupt ceaselessly, making new rocks, new land, new islands. I am the earth eater, the land maker.

Mount Kīlauea in south-east Hawaii is Pele's home and is the world's most active volcano. People leave piles of stones as offerings to honour and appease Pele. But do not pick up a piece of Pele's lava and put it in your pocket, even the tiniest piece will only bring you bad luck.

Mistress of Magic,
Speaker of Spells

Egypt

Isis is more intelligent than all the countless gods, and more rebellious than a million men. She is the Mistress of Magic, Speaker of Spells. She knows spells to heal, spells to kill, spells to break hearts, spells to ignite old flames. Her breath carries enchantments that destroy sickness, her mouth forms words that repel pain. She is a queen with a headdress shaped like a gilded throne. She is a goddess with a headdress in the form of a solar disk sitting between two horns. Around her hips is a blood-red girdle. She tightens the knot of the vermillion sash, transforms into other beings and journeys to other worlds. She opens her arms and they become wings. She is kite, falcon, swallow, vulture.

Isis knew all spells, except one. She did not know the secret magic name of Ra. If she could possess Ra's secret name then she would have the power of life over death. Isis watched Ra on his endless journey, travelling across the sky in his boat of a million years. In the morning he was a golden-haired boy, in the middle of the day a blazing warrior. Isis waited for evening. Ra became an old man with bright white hair and began to dribble. She watched the potent spit pool on Ra's lip, drip from his mouth and drop onto the earth. Isis scooped up Ra's fertile spit. She kneaded the spit with mud and shaped it into a snake, a poisonous serpent.

Isis placed the snake at the crossroads, the place where Ra changed from warrior to old man. The next day, as Ra's golden hair began to turn white, the snake reared up and bit him.

Poison coursed through Ra's body and he called out, 'What has bitten me?'

Ra's jaws trembled, his body quaked and he fell to the ground. The poison spread as swiftly as the Nile in flood. Gods rushed to his side but their medicines and charms could not stop the poison. Ra cried, 'I did not make this! I created everything, yet I have been bitten by something I did not create.'

Isis appeared, 'All Father are you ill? Perhaps I can help?'

She opened her arms, 'I made the snake and only I can heal you. I will drive away the poison if you tell me your secret name. Reveal your name and I will save you.'

Ra groaned, sweating and shivering, 'I am He Who Opens His Eye. I am Bringer of Light. I am Binder of Mountains. I am Khepri in the morning, Ra at noon, Atum at dusk.'

Isis towered above him, 'Those are the names by which you are known. I want the name which is unknown. Tell me your secret name.'

Ra clutched his chest, he was on fire, the poison spread towards his heart. 'I cannot hold!' he cried.

'Then tell me your secret name.'

Ra mumbled, 'Place your heart over my heart. My secret name will pass from heart to heart. And you must promise to pass my name to your son, Horus, when he is born. And he too must pass it on, so all your ancestors will hold my name in their hearts.'

Isis knelt and pressed her chest against Ra's chest. The secret name of Ra passed from heart to heart and entered Isis. The Mistress Of Magic rose to her feet, the Speaker Of Spells raised her arms and uttered, 'Ra lives and the poison dies! The poison dies and Ra lives! I made you serpent and I send you away. Snake leave Ra. Poison fall to the ground.'

These were the words of the great Goddess Isis. Ra stopped trembling, his jaw stopped shaking and his limbs became still. Ra was calm, he could breathe again and his strength returned. Ra climbed into his boat of a million years and continued on his endless journey.

Isis needed nothing more. She knew Ra's secret magic name and possessed the power of life over death. She was the divine magician who knew the spell to bring back the dead. And she knew she would need it, knew she would use it to bring her brother, her lover, her husband, her king, Osiris back to life. She lowered her arms and felt the shape and weight of her baby son, Horus, yet to come.

The spells of Isis were written down by Thoth, God of Writing. Thoth used his pointed black beak as a writing tool, pressing it into clay tablets that still exist today. The spells of Isis became part of the Book of the Dead, the heart of Egyptian ritual practices, spells that bring the dead through the underworld to eternal life. But Ra's hidden name was never written down and remains a secret, like all the best magic spells.

This story was believed to have healing powers. The spoken narrative was itself a spell for repelling poison. If you were bitten by a snake then reciting this story over an image of Isis would heal you. The story could also be written onto the hand of a wounded patient. If they licked off the words, the poison would leave their body and they would be cured.

In Ancient Egypt many of narratives about Isis were used as incantations to promote healing, cure the sick and restore good health.

Anahita

Iran

Pure Mighty Moist One, Anahita, Goddess of the Waters, is the heavenly river and from her all streams, rivers, lakes, seas, oceans flow. Maiden Anahita is the immaculate source of all the water that circulates around the world. She is the Great Spring flowing from on high that gives us all life.

Is she a snowy mountain top whose icy meltwater runs into all rivers? Or is she a brilliant white star circling in the heavens bringing rain? No! She is an unstoppable warrior. She sits astride her tiger or stands in her chariot, dressed in a gold embroidered gown with gold laced boots and heavy ornaments shining on her chest. She holds the sun in one hand and the moon in the other. Her chariot is pulled by her four horses Wind, Rain, Cloud and Sleet. She charges forward, racing across the sky, a warrior riding to war. And she always wins. Her power is an unrelenting, ever-increasing force. She gushes, surges, floods. She is the generator of crops, of milk, of children. Her ceaseless flow brings healing.

Immerse yourself in her and be purified. Bathe in her and be regenerated. Drink in her wisdom.

Anahita was part of the Zoroastrian pantheon. She was linked to the planet Venus, is often represented as a star and is connected to the goddesses Ishtar, Isis and Venus.

Durga Demon-Slayer

India

Durga is virgin, lover, mother and all warrior. She was born from pure rage. A rage that filled the gods when demonic forces overwhelmed heaven and earth. Demon Mahisa had chanted the spell of immortality for a thousand years and accrued so much power he could not be killed by god or man. Mahisa turned himself into the monstrous Buffalo Demon, charged into heaven, tossed the gods down to earth and took their place. Rivers ran dry, fire could not be put out, stars reversed their movements across the sky and gods wandered lost over earth like mere humans.

Rage rose up inside the gods and flames of fury shot from their eyes. Their fury fused into a blazing fire that turned into a woman; a warrior maiden with golden skin that lit up the universe. The anger of the gods created the fiery Goddess Durga! The Flaming One threw back her head and laughed. 'The Buffalo Demon cannot be killed by god or man. The fool forgot about woman!'

Durga laughed louder. She shook her ten arms, or was it eight, sixteen or eighteen arms? Nothing is certain with Durga. Not her multiple forms or even her name. Durga, Demon-Slayer, the Supreme One was more dangerous than all the gods and demons put together and she was born to kill. Each god gave her their sacred symbol of divine power: Indra, God of Sky – a thunderbolt; Vayu, Lord of Wind – a bow; Suraya, the Sun – arrows; Vishnu, Protector – his silver discus; Varuna, God of Water – a conch shell; Agni, God of Fire – flaming spears; Shiva, Destroyer – his pointed trident; Yama, God of Death – his noose; Kala, Lord of Time – a sword. And Brahma, the Creator, gave a drinking cup always full of blood-red wine, or was it the sweet nectar of immortality? The gods dressed Durga in shining garments that would never wear out, placed gold around her neck and rings on each of her fingers. And they gave her a yellow tiger from the Himalayas as a mount. Durga climbed onto her tiger and rode into battle to fight Mahisa.

And the gods cried, 'Victory to the Mother!'

The Buffalo Demon heard a rumbling sound. He sent his army of demons to investigate.

'It's just a woman!' they cried.

The demons swarmed over the goddess. She stood still, her face calm, then her multiple arms rotated. Her weapons flashed like cosmic fireworks. She sliced serenely through the demons, smiling peacefully while all around was total destruction and corpses covered the earth. Durga sighed and her sigh turned into an army of warrior maidens, who marched across the world slaying every demon in sight. Durga destroyed Mahisa's army and the Buffalo Demon was left alone.

Mahisa changed his form, he became a giant man and tried to seduce the goddess.

'There is no love,' laughed Durga, 'only war! And I have been created to kill you!'

She loosed an arrow and struck the demon's chest. Mahisa changed again and became an elephant the size of a mountain. Durga sliced off his trunk. Mahisa turned back into a buffalo.

'You're only a woman,' he bellowed.

The goddess whirled her noose and caught the buffalo by its horns. The buffalo stamped and snorted. Durga raised her magic drinking cup. 'Bellow away,' she cried. 'When I've finished drinking, you'll never bellow again.'

She drank, wiped blood-red wine from her lips, leapt on top of the buffalo and pinned his neck to the ground. Mahisa was helpless. Durga lifted her trident and stabbed him in the heart. He roared and a hideous creature emerged from his mouth. The demon's true form came out of his own mouth! The goddess drew Time's sword. 'Your time is up!' she said. And the All-Comprehending-One sliced off the demon's true head.

Mahisa had been killed by a woman. Order was restored. Rivers flowed, fires went out, stars followed their correct course and the gods returned to heaven. Durga's ten arms became still. She closed her eyes, smiled peacefully. And waited for the next demon.

Raktavija was so deadly he could not be killed. If a single drop of his blood was shed it would turn into a thousand demons and no one had been able to destroy him. Durga furrowed her brow and a third eye appeared in her forehead. Her third eye opened and out sprang Kali, she who dissolves all evil. She had blue skin, three red eyes, four arms, a necklace of skulls, a skirt of severed hands, yellow tusks and a long, red tongue. Kali's three eyes could see into the past, present and future. She was wisdom and warrior combined and the most terrifying goddess of all. 'I arise to protect creation!' she cried.

Kali picked up Raktavija, lifted him high into the sky so not a drop of his blood would spill upon earth, then sank her tusks into his body. She drank his blood dry and threw his bloodless carcass down to earth. Kali was covered in blood. She licked up the blood and it filled her with lust for more. Her four arms began to whirl, she started killing birds, animals, humans and drinking their blood. Her crazed slaughter was unstoppable.

She would have destroyed the entire universe, but Shiva, God of Destruction, and her husband, lay down on the blood-soaked battlefield. In the centre of the carnage Kali stood on top of Shiva and suddenly woke up. Kali remembered who she was, and instantly she was absorbed back into Durga. Then Durga herself turned into Parvati, the peaceful daughter of the Himalayas and Shiva's wife.

Durga Demon-Slayer is the magic of illusion that creates the world. Even Shiva cannot comprehend her. Compared to the vast sea of being that is Durga, the other gods are like drops of water left behind in the hollow imprint of a cow's hoof. And just as it is impossible for those tiny drops of water to understand the vastness of the sea, so it is impossible for the gods to know Durga. Honour the Mistress of the Universe with flowers, perfume, milk, gold. Her arrows destroy the demonic fear in our minds. Her eyes see in all directions, giving us fierce hearts. Remember Durga and you can conquer your demons. Know Durga and you can actualise your power. Hail Supremely Radiant Durga, she alone can remove suffering from the world.

Durga has many complex, wonderful intertwined stories that are beyond the scope of this book, including the story of how she takes her name Durga from a demon! She appears in many forms with different names: Sati; Parvati; Gauri; Uma; Chandi; Devi; Durga; Kali. She transforms from loving to fierce and back again in a cosmic dance with her beloved Shiva. Prayers and rituals to Durga are important in India and other parts of the world, and it is said whoever recites them will never be alone.

Pallas Athena

Greece

Athena let out a warrior cry, 'I am Goddess of Wisdom, Goddess of War. I am thought brought forth. I am wisdom and cunning combined. I am triumphant!'

Athena was born from Zeus's head. After Zeus had satisfied himself with Titaness Metis, the giantess conceived and roared, 'I will give birth to a son who will take your place!'

Zeus remembered his own father, Ouranos, swallowing his children when they threatened to overthrow him. So Zeus did the same, he opened his mouth and swallowed Metis whole. The giantess disappeared into the darkness, never to be seen again. But her baby did not die, it grew inside its father. Until Zeus had a terrible headache. He writhed in agony and begged Hephaistos to help him. The Blacksmith God took up his axe and struck Zeus on the forehead. Zeus's head split open and out sprang a woman with fierce eyes, dressed in a suit of armour! Athena leapt to the ground with a battle cry and Mount Olympus trembled.

'At least you're not a boy!' said Zeus. 'And you will be tamed.'

Athena was given to the River God Triton. He schooled Athena with his own daughter, Pallas. The two maidens learned the skills of combat together on the banks of the river and became close friends. One day they were practising spear throwing.

Athena hurled her spear, Pallas shifted slightly and the spear struck her in the chest. The maiden fell to the ground dead. Athena knelt beside her friend and wept, 'I will build a temple to you my sister. I will wear your name maiden, weaving it always with mine.'

Pallas Athena turned herself into an owl. She swooped over earth looking for a place to build her temple. She landed on a high outcrop of rocks, 'I claim this place!' she cried, and an olive tree sprang from the ground.

Suddenly a golden trident landed beside the tree and water gushed from the dry rocks. Poseidon, God of the Sea appeared, 'I claim this place!' he cried.

Athena and Poseidon argued about who could claim the dusty rocks. Until Zeus announced, 'Let the people choose.'

'Choose me!' cried Athena. 'I will give you olives to eat, oil for cooking, light for your lamps and I will protect you fiercely.'

'Choose me!' said Poseidon. 'I will give you water to drink, your nets will be full of fish and your ships will always arrive safe to shore.'

'Olive tree or salty sea?' cried Zeus.

The women wanted olive oil, the men successful fishing. The votes were counted. And there was one more woman than there were men. Pallas Athena won. She claimed the rock and the people named their city after her – Athens. 'It is war, Father!' cried Athena. 'No son will take your place, but a daughter will!' Athena built her temple high on top of the rock, with columns and steps, doorways and halls. A huge statue was made of Pallas Athena covered in ivory and gold, seven times taller than a human being.

'Are you watching Father?' cried Athena.

Hephaistos came to the temple demanding a reward for helping give birth to the goddess.

'For your hard work you may enjoy me for one night,' said Pallas Athena. 'Lie beneath my tree tonight and I will come to you.'

When night fell, Hephaistos stretched out beneath the olive tree. He saw Athena approaching, dressed as a bride and was filled with lust. Athena lay beside him and Hephaistos rolled towards her, opened his arms to embrace her and there was nothing but dust. The goddess had vanished. Hephaistos could not contain his desire, he groaned and his semen fell onto the dry earth. A boy, Erichthonius, was born. And this divine child became the King of Athens.

Pallas Athena's power spread, but there was one thing that she was missing. When Poseidon pursued maiden Medusa into Athena's own temple and raped her, Athena was watching. She punished the poor girl, turning Medusa's long, golden curls into green, writhing snakes and Medusa's lovely dark eyes blood red. Medusa became a monster, a gorgon who could turn anything to stone. Then Athena helped hero Perseus kill Medusa. 'Use my shield as a mirror.'

Perseus saw the terrible reflection of Medusa in the shield and Athena guided his hand so he sliced off the gorgon's head. It fell to the ground and with a flash of silver, something rose up out of Medusa's neck, the silver-winged horse, Pegasus. Beauty had been set free and flew away. But Athena took Medusa's head and pressed it into the centre of her shield. Terror and rage turned to bronze, Medusa's power was hers, Pallas Athena was complete, 'I will never be tamed. Do you hear me, Father?

The Goddess of War set about changing the course of history by helping and hindering all the heroes. She aided Argos, Bellerophon, Heracles, Orestes, Odysseus, Achilles, Laertes, Telemachus. Each hero thought winning or losing was within his own power but it was always what the goddess wished for. Pallas Athena appeared on battlefields, in chariots, tents, temples, palaces, on horseback and in disguise. She gave advice, guided thoughts, appeared in dreams, made war plans, placed weapons in warriors' hands, encouraged revenge, turned families against each other and enemies to face each other.

'I am lightning. I am the roar of battle. I am the sound of swords clashing. It is war, Father,' said the Goddess of Wisdom. 'War of the mind!'

The Goddess Athena appears in many Greek myths and has a major role in the Odyssey.

Amaterasu Sun Goddess

Japan

We cannot live without you Amaterasu. Heaven-illuminating spirit warm us, fill the world with light and heat, never hide behind clouds, do not disappear again.

Amaterasu, Sun Goddess, has red-gold hair, a luminous face and a shining necklace. When she appears rice grows, buds open, flowers bloom, people come out of their homes, take off their coats and turn their faces towards her.

The Sun Goddess has two brothers and there is always conflict between them. Tsuki, Moon God, is pale and dreamy with silver hair. He took up too much space and Amaterasu would not share the sky with him. She banished Tsuki to the night sky and he only came out when he was sure his sister was asleep.

Amaterasu's other brother, Susa, Storm God, has blue-black hair and a terrible temper. He had no home and raged over earth, weeping and wailing. He howled around mountains, shaking trees, rattling windows, tearing tiles from roofs. When Susa appeared people pulled on their coats, covered their heads and ran for shelter.

'I am not welcome anywhere,' wailed Susa.

Susa marched into the sky to live with his sister and brother. As he strode, clouds rumbled, lightning flashed and rocks crashed into the sea. Amaterasu heard the noise and prepared for battle, arrayed herself for deadly conflict. The Sun Goddess bound her hair into two warrior knots, tied her robe into trousers, slung a quiver of a thousand arrows on her back, brandished her bow and placed her feet in a warrior stance. She stood so strongly, so firmly, she sank into the earth up to her thighs. Susa saw his sister dressed like a soldier.

'I have not come to fight, sister. I have come to stay.'

'If you come in peace,' said Amaterasu, 'then give me your sword.'

Susa pulled his sword from his belt. His sister snapped the sword into three pieces, put the pieces in her mouth, chewed them up, spat them into the sky and three new stars appeared. 'Now you may be my guest,' she said.

Susa walked with his sister through her fields of waving rice. He tossed his blue-black hair and torrents of water washed the rice away. He entered her golden halls, lifted his hand and wind blasted her freshly hung curtains, ripping them to shreds. Amaterasu was incensed and Susa promised to behave. But he could not help himself, Susa was the Storm God, it was his nature, and just as storm clouds cover the sun so Susa upset his sister. He pissed in her shrine room, then defecated on her throne. When Amaterasu was with her sun maidens in the weaving hall, weaving the sacred garments of the gods, there was a loud bang. A chunk of ceiling crashed to the floor and Susa peered through a hole in the roof. He roared with laughter and lowered a rope through the hole. Bound to the rope was the body of a dead horse, freshly flayed with a backward flaying. It was an act of utter disrespect. The sun maidens screamed in horror, their shuttles shot from their hands, wounding them in the source-places of their female power. Blood flowed, staining their gowns red. Amaterasu was outraged, 'How dare you dishonour my maidens. I never want to see your face again!'

The Sun Goddess gathered up her robes and ran out of the hall, over the fields, into the forest, to a cave. She ran inside the cave and rolled a great rock across the entrance. The world was plunged into darkness. The sun disappeared without trace and a never-ending night covered earth. The sun did not rise. Tsuki lit the sky at night, but the alternation of day and night stopped. Rice did not grow, everyone was cold and spirits and ghosts freely roamed the world. The gods and goddesses tried to roll the rock aside and couldn't. They begged Amaterasu to come out of the cave, but she wouldn't.

Earth was dying. The gods had to bring Amaterasu back. The Blacksmith God forged an eight-sided mirror. He polished the surface of the mirror until it shone. The gods hung the mirror in the branches of a cherry tree beside the cave. The mirror gleamed like an eight-petalled silver flower. The gods decorated the tree with curved jewels and blue and white streamers, and placed a freshly woven silken robe at the roots of the tree. Then they summoned the night birds, the crickets and a rooster. The singing birds of the eternal night sang and sang, the crickets chirped and the cockerel crowed without stopping. Amaterasu heard them and cried, 'I am not coming out!'

Uzume, Goddess of Dancing, appeared, holding a spear and wearing a headdress hung with jewels that tinkled as she moved. Uzume began to dance, lifting her feet, turning her body, moving her arms. The gods clapped and Uzume drummed her feet. Inside the cave Amaterasu could hear the noise.

'I am never coming out!' she called. Uzume began to whirl, her robe twirling. She loosened her robe, bared her breasts and tugged her nipples. The gods cheered and Amaterasu listened.

'I am not ever coming out!' she cried. Uzume twirled faster, she lowered her robe further, swirling her belly and shaking her thighs. Then she dropped the robe and opened her legs, opened her legs wider still, revealing for all to see the rosy source place of her femininity. Gods and goddesses roared with laughter.

'Why are you laughing?' cried Amaterasu.

She could not help herself, she was curious and the Sun Goddess rolled the rock aside a tiny bit and peeped out. A streak of light lit up the dark sky and everyone gasped, and the first rays of dawn have taken our breath away ever since. A beam of light fell upon Uzume.

'Why are you laughing?' asked the Sun Goddess.

'My Lady,' said Uzume, 'we are celebrating because we have found someone who is beautiful!'

And Uzume pointed at the mirror. Amaterasu saw the reflection of a shining face, 'Oh! Yes! How beautiful!' she said.

Amaterasu pushed the rock aside and stepped out of the cave. The world was filled with light and heat. The gods quickly pulled a rope made of rice-straw across the cave entrance so the Sun Goddess could not go back inside. Amaterasu walked towards the dazzling face, and it was so bright she had to shield her eyes.

'Who is she?' asked Amaterasu.

'Sun Goddess,' said Uzume, 'who in the whole world could be more beautiful than yourself?'

Uzume dressed Amaterasu in the silk robe. 'Heaven-Illuminating spirit do not leave us, never hide behind clouds, do not disappear again. We cannot live without you.'

Amaterasu returned to her palace and order was restored to the world. Rice grew, buds opened, flowers bloomed and people took off their coats and turned their faces towards the sun. But Amaterasu found Susa sitting in a puddle of water sulking.

'You need a palace of your own,' she said. 'Where you can make as much mess and noise as you like!'

And so she sent Susa to the ocean. Clouds of foam arose from the sea to welcome the Storm God to his new palace, and Susa has been crashing and pounding in the ocean ever since. Amaterasu gave the eight-sided mirror to the first emperor. It was placed inside a bag, and each emperor placed the mirror inside another bag. The mirror still exists, inside bags and bags and bags that get ever older and more frail. Today the mirror rests on the altar of a Shinto shrine. Amaterasu descends into the mirror when she wants to make herself visible to humans.

And the mirror says to all who look into it, 'Who could be more beautiful than yourself.'

This myth is the heart of Shinto religion, and my version is freely drawn from the ancient Japanese manuscripts 'Kojiki' and 'Nihongi'. Decorating trees to keep the sun alight during the dark of winter is a tradition in many parts of the world. And drumming, beating pots and making a noise to scare away bad spirits during an eclipse to bring back the sun is something that happens across the world.

Sekhmet Lioness

Egypt

She was born from anger, roaring and shaking her golden mane. It happened when Sun God Ra looked down on Earth and saw that human beings had become so absorbed by life they no longer followed the sacred laws. Seduced by the world, they had forgotten Maat, the life-preserving justice that had been bestowed upon them, and they no longer cared about the sustenance and order of the universe. Fury flashed across Ra's eye, boiling anger rose up, jumped out of his eye and turned into a woman, the Goddess Sekhmet. She was wearing a red dress with thick, golden hair hanging down her back. She had the head of a lioness and between her tall ears was a sun disc encircled by a cobra.

Sekhmet stretched her powerful limbs and bounded across Earth. She pounced on foolish humans, biting and scratching, ripping and tearing. The lioness drank blood and devoured flesh. The Scarlet Lady hunted down every living thing, seizing her prey and gorging on it. There was so much blood that the dust and mud of Egypt turned red. Ra watched the carnage and ordered Sekhmet to cease. But the goddess was so consumed by lust, her rage was uncontrollable.

Sekhmet was destroying life on Earth. Born from the Eye of Ra, the Sun God had to stop the force he had brought into being. He mixed beer with pomegranate juice, staining the beer red. He poured seven thousand jugs of scarlet beer into the River Nile, dying it deep red. Sekhmet ran to the river of blood. She knelt on the river bank and cupped her hands, filling them with red liquid and gulping it down. The beer calmed her fury and soothed her passion. Sekhmet stretched out, she lay on her belly and put her muzzle to the river. She lapped up the red beer and her rage relaxed, her anger softened, her eyes became heavy and warm sleep swept over her. Sekhmet was so intoxicated she slept for three days. When she finally woke her blood lust had dissipated. Sekhmet Lioness was calm and humanity was saved. And precious Maat, life-preserving justice, had been returned to the world. But the Scarlet Lady had been brought into existence and Sekhmet Lioness is ready to pounce the moment humans forget the sacred laws of existence.

Lilith, Goddess of Night

Hebrew

Lilith is half of us.

Lilith had long, dark, curly hair, dazzling eyes and a mouth like a pomegranate cut open. She was created when Yahweh separated the male and female parts of the first human being. That first human was made from a handful of dust and contained within itself both male and female. The first human lived in the Garden of Eden with all the animals. Each animal had a mate and the animals spent their time gambolling and coupling. The first human looked around but could not find a mate.

The human complained to Yahweh, 'Every living thing has a mate except me. I'm lonely. I want someone like me.'

'Are we here already?' said Yahweh, separating the male and female parts to create Adam and Lilith.

Adam was bewitched by Lilith and fell in love. But even though they were living in paradise, Adam and Lilith could not stop arguing. Because whenever they had sex, Adam always wanted to lie on top.

'I want to lie on top,' said Lilith.

'No!' said Adam. 'I lie on top. That is how it is done.'

'Why?' protested Lilith. 'I am made from the same dust as you. I am your equal. I am half of you. I will lie on top when I want to!'

But Adam did not agree, he pressed Lilith down and tried to force her to his will. Lilith was filled with rage, she scratched Adam, tore at his face, pushed him aside and leapt to her feet. She opened her arms and shouted strange words, she uttered the secret, magic, ineffable name of Yahweh, the name that no one knew or had ever heard! Black feathers burst from her arms, her feet became claws and she soared into the air and flew away.

Adam complained again, 'You made her all wrong. She has left me.'

'Of course,' sighed Yahweh, and sent three angels, Senoy, Sansenoy and Semangelof, to fetch her back.

They found Lilith by the shores of the Red Sea with wings and claws, her body covered in hair and scales. Part woman, part bird, part snake. Lilith had become the Goddess of Night. She was surrounded by demons. She was coupling with demons and giving birth to hundreds of demon babies, all girls!

'You are required to return,' said the angels.

'Never!' cried Lilith.

'Then we will kill a hundred of your babies every day,' said the angels.

'Kill away!' screamed Lilith. 'I would rather be childless than return to that man.'

Yahweh set about making a new mate for Adam. 'Watch!' he cried. 'You will like her better if you see how she is created.'

So Adam watched as bones, tissues, muscles, veins were wrapped in skin. He saw hair going on in all the right places, but the sight of all the flesh and blood made Adam throw up. He was repulsed and refused to have anything to do with the woman. Adam's second wife wandered off alone into the forest. No one knows her name, but she still lives wild among the trees waiting for all women to find her.

'Creating looks easy,' said Yahweh. 'Until your creation gets a mind of its own and turns out to be fussy. This time I will put Adam to sleep so he won't see anything. And I will take a bit of Adam himself to make his mate, so that he feels related to her.'

Yahweh put Adam to sleep, pulled out one of his ribs and made Eve. Yahweh plaited her hair, dressed her in jewels and silks and over every part of her body chanted, 'Be chaste, be chaste, be chaste.' But it had no effect, because woman already was! Then Yahweh got some angels to play harps and drums and Adam woke to a beguiling vision, and fell in love a second time.

Adam and Eve made their home in the Garden of Eden. In the centre of the garden they found two huge trees. The Tree of Life with four rivers flowing from its roots, rivers of milk, oil, honey and wine. And the Tree of Knowledge covered in sweet-smelling fruit.

'Eat anything,' said Yahweh. 'Except the fruit from the Tree of Knowledge.'

Adam and Eve lived in bliss. Until the Goddess of Night spread her dark wings and flew over the garden. She whispered, 'Enjoy it now! It won't always be this way.'

Lilith changed her shape, turned into a snake and slithered into the garden. She coiled herself around the Tree of Knowledge. And as Eve passed by the snake hissed, 'Eat! It's delicious.'

'That fruit is poisonous, if we eat we will die,' said Eve.

'That's just a story!' hissed the snake. 'You are forbidden to eat this fruit, because if you do, you will become like god!'

The snake opened her mouth and bit the fruit. 'See ... I am unharmed.'

Eve breathed in the sweet smell of the fruit.

'Try,' said the snake.

Eve stretched out her hand, picked a fruit and put it to her mouth. The fruit burst open. It tasted quite different from any other fruit. Eve ate and a thought flashed through her mind, a thought she had never had before, 'Who am I? What am I doing here?'

The snake laughed, 'Knowledge!'

Eve suddenly saw that the snake was a woman with wings and claws. She was afraid, plucked another fruit and ran to Adam.

Adam stared at Eve, she looked quite different. Her outer skin of light, like a pearly shell, had fallen away and underneath she was naked. Her skin looked soft, warm and smooth. Eve offered Adam the fruit. He took it and held it in his hand. He knew he should not eat the fruit but he gazed at Eve longingly. Holding the fruit, he wrestled with himself for three hours and in the end he said, 'You are so lovely, I would rather be with you than live without you.' Adam bit the fruit and his skin of light fell away. Adam and Eve ate, then satisfied, fell asleep in each other's arms. The next morning the garden was not the same. Flowers had wilted, blossoms blew about in the wind, plants had withered and fruit had dropped to the ground. Death had come. Death had come to the garden. Adam and Eve felt afraid, and suddenly knew they were naked. They reached up into the trees to pick leaves to cover their bodies, but the trees drove them away, battering them with their branches. Only the Tree of Knowledge protected them, letting them pick its leaves, admiring their choice of wisdom rather than immortality.

Yahweh had seen everything and Adam and Eve were cast out of the Garden of Eden. An angel stood at the entrance of paradise guarding it with a fiery revolving sword. As they left, Adam turned to the angel and asked, 'Can we ever come back?'

'Yes,' said the angel, 'when the Oil of Mercy has been granted.'

Adam and Eve walked away and their feet burned the ground, scorching it black, leaving a trail of black footprints behind them. They wandered into the desert, where Eve gave birth to sons Cain and Abel. But for those first children life was not eternal. Death had come into the world and there was nothing a mother or father could do to prevent it. The fruit had been picked.

Howling and shrieking, the Goddess of Night flew around the world at the head of a host of demons. She is the Queen of Demons and couples with demons, giving birth to baby girls, endlessly filling the world with female demons! Senoy, Sansenoy and Semangelof kill a hundred of her demon babies every day. But there are always more demons! And in revenge, Lilith flies into bedrooms, climbs on top of men while they are asleep and rides them, taking her pleasure on top! Then she creeps into the nursery, tickling babies, making them gurgle and roll about. When a baby gets that tangle of hair on the back of its head, you know that Lilith has been visiting. Sometimes the Goddess of Night puts spells on the baby or picks them up and sucks them dry. Parents recite charms and hang amulets above the cradle to protect the child. The amulets have images of the three angels banishing Lilith, or images of the goddess in shackles and chains and the words 'Adam and Eve – Lilith out'. But Lilith is half of us. She is within us all and the Goddess of Night can never be banished. So lie on top, women! Hunt down knowledge. Pick fruit. Go to the very top of the tree. Let Lilith fly free.

Lilith has been linked to goddesses Inanna and Ishtar. Sumerian cylinder seals and Mesopotamian plaques repeatedly show images of a goddess with a tree, a snake or a bird, sometimes she has claws and wings, or is accompanied by lions and owls. This bird-footed, winged goddess spread from Sumerian myth into Jewish folklore. Lilith is found in Kabbalistic texts, in the Talmud's 'Zohar' and 'Targum Sheni'. She then spread into European medieval folktales and folklore. Many medieval manuscripts depict the serpent in the Garden of Eden as a woman. In the Christian text 'The Golden Legend', you can find the story about how Adam's son Seth returns to the Garden of Eden and finds out what the Oil of Mercy is.

Aphrodite, Foam Born

Greece

The Golden One was made of desire and born from her father's testicles! Her father was Ouranos, Sky. Ouranos coupled with Mother Earth, Gaia, and Earth gave birth to a world of children. Sky was threatened by his children, afraid that they would overthrow him. So he pushed his children underground, buried them deep inside Mother Earth. Gaia groaned in pain and fury and urged her children to rebel. She formed a sickle of black flint within her body. Her eldest son, Kronos, took the knife. Kronos reached up towards his father, flashed the blade, sliced his father's testicles off and hurled them into the sea! The deed was done. Ouranos could not produce any more children.

But that was not the end of the testicles! The testicles bobbed on the waves, floated out to sea and white foam gathered around them. The foam frothed and bubbled, foamed and formed into a woman. She was a marvellous beauty with glistening skin and tumbling hair. She was desire embodied, Aphrodite, Foam Born.

Aphrodite drifted on the briny water. There was splash and a spirit appeared beside her. Nerites, a triton of the sea, admired her, circling her, splashing her playfully, 'You are a pearl!'

Aphrodite was enchanted, desire rose inside her and she wrapped her legs around Nerites. They became lovers, plunging and diving together in the salty sea.

When they reached shallow waters, Aphrodite offered Nerites her hand. 'I must take my place among the gods and goddesses,' she said, 'and you will be beside me.'

Nerites shook his head, 'I cannot leave the sea, this is where I belong.'

'But you belong to love now!' said Aphrodite.

She clasped his hand. And as their fingers twined together, water trickled through her fingers and Nerites vanished. And in the palm of Aphrodite's hand was a perfect cockleshell.

Aphrodite climbed into the shell and was carried over the waves to the shore of an island. The Golden One, Goddess of Love, Aphrodite, Foam Born stepped onto land. Love had arrived. And wherever she went, she spread desire.

Some say the island was Kythira, some say Cyprus. There are important shrines to Aphrodite on both islands. Pilgrims would honour Aphrodite with cockleshells, a tradition that continued into Christian practice. And a type of bivalve shell is known as a Venus Clam.

Sisters in Love and Death

Mesopotamia

One sister lived above, the other sister lived below. Ishtar, Goddess of Love and War, was honoured in the Great Above. Ereshkigal, Goddess of the Underworld, ruled the Great Below. Ishtar, Goddess of Love, delighted in her vulva, relished in its power and not even a hundred and twenty thousand lovers could satisfy her! But Ishtar was the Goddess of War and she did not treat her lovers well. She struck the many-coloured roller bird and broke his wing. She dug seven pits and buried the lion of tremendous strength. She whipped and spurred the magnificent stallion. She turned the shepherd into a wolf, and her father's gardener into a frog. Ishtar aroused such desire, there was only one who rejected her and that was Gilgamesh, the great hero. When Ishtar said, 'Be my lover.'

Gilgamesh replied, 'To be loved like you loved the others? No!'

Ereshkigal longed for the unrestrained passion of her sister, but she was sent down to the Great Below, to the Land of the Dead, to rule in the cold darkness. Lovers and consorts visited her, and left as soon as they could; no one wanted to stay in the underworld. The Queen of the Dead languished alone. The Goddess of the Underworld forgot to take care of herself. She let her nails grow as long as copper rakes, leeches crawled through her matted hair, spiders wove webs over her body and her face became as pale as the ghosts that surrounded her.

When they were maidens, the sisters had both loved the same young man, Tammuz, God of Spring. He was so fresh and unspoiled they both wanted him. It was Ishtar who had won Tammuz, he had become her first sweetheart, the lover of her youth. Tammuz was the one love that Ishtar would never harm. Ishtar had not stopped loving Tammuz. And neither had Ereshkigal.

A long time after the Great Above had moved away from the Great Below, the rains stopped. Sweltering heat pressed over the land like a furnace. The earth was parched, rivers dried up, buildings cracked, animals died. Fields of sesame and barley failed, dates and olives shrivelled and fell from the trees. Tammuz suffered like the land. He lay parched in the shade, breathless, thirsty. Ishtar came to his side, took his head in her lap and wet his lips with water. But the heat was too much, and like the plants that had wilted, Tammuz withered and died. Ishtar held him in her arms and tried to revive him, but his soul had left his body. It floated down to the underworld, to the palace of Ereshkigal to sleep for eternity with all the other souls of the dead. Ishtar led the world in lamentation. Desolation fell upon the earth, the ground turned to dust, nothing grew. Ishtar declared, 'I will go to the Great Below and bring him back. For Tammuz I will descend to the Land of the Dead.'

Ishtar's female companions tried to dissuade her, 'No one returns from that dark place.'

But Ishtar insisted. She dressed in her robe of rippling tiers. She braided her hair and fixed her crown, shaped like a mountain between two horns, in place. She put on her jewels and slung bow and arrows on her back. 'If I do not return in three days mourn my death and perform the funeral rite for me.' Then Ishtar descended.

From the Great Above she set her mind on the Great Below. She followed the path of ashes down to the Land of No-Return. She travelled the road from which there is no way back. She went to the house where there is no light, to the place where the dwellers eat dust and clay. Ishtar descended down a narrow track, deeper and deeper into darkness. She descended all the way to the entrance of the underworld.

There were seven gates, each gate locked and covered in ancient dust. No one had entered the gates for a very long time. Ishtar called out to the gatekeeper, 'Open the gates or I will smash them down and break the locks. Open the gates or I will let out the dead so that the dead outnumber the living.'

Neti, the gatekeeper appeared behind the seventh gate. He held up a lantern, 'Why you have come Lady?'

'I have come for Tammuz. I have come to wake him up.'

'Let me speak to Queen Ereshkigal.'

The gatekeeper hurried to the Queen of the Dead. Ereshkigal sat in the gloomy dark on a high stone throne surrounded by ghosts.

'What does my sister want here?' she cried. 'Where there is nothing to eat but dust and clay? Why is she visiting me now? After all these years of neglect, of leaving me alone? She cannot have Tammuz, he belongs to me now. And doesn't she realise that if she wants to come to my house she must be treated like all who enter the underworld? Let her in, but she must follow the ancient rites!'

The gatekeeper returned and shook his keys, 'You must follow the rites of the underworld. Leave your weapons outside and you may enter.'

Ishtar put down her quivers and bow. The gatekeeper unlocked the first gate. 'Take off your crown.'

Ishtar resisted, 'I am a goddess.'

The gatekeeper insisted, so Ishtar took off her crown and stepped through the first gate. Neti stood by the second gate and held out his hand. 'Your earrings.'

Ishtar removed them and he opened the second gate. At the third gate Neti requested, 'Your necklace.'

At the fourth gate he said, 'Your brooches … all of them.'

At the fifth gate, 'The jewelled sandals from your feet.'

Ishtar stepped through the fifth gate with bare feet.

At the sixth gate the gatekeeper said, 'Your belt of stars.'

And at the seventh gate, 'Your robe.'

'You have removed my divinity,' replied Ishtar. 'And now you want to take my humanity too.'

Reluctantly, she removed her gown and passed through the seventh gate into the underworld without weapons, jewels or clothes.

Ishtar stood before her sister naked. 'Are you happy now that you have taken everything I came with?'

'Why didn't you visit me before?' asked Ereshkigal. 'I am so lonely down here with no one to speak to, nothing to enjoy.'

'Forgive me sister,' said Ishtar. 'I beg for your help. I have come for Tammuz, the world and I need him.'

'Tammuz is dead,' replied Ereshkigal. 'And the dead belong to the dead.'

Ereshkigal's face turned yellow, her lips went black and she fixed on Ishtar the eye of death.

'And this is what becomes of the dead.'

Ereshkigal called out to a servant, 'Tie her up. Unleash the diseases.'

Ishtar was bound and gagged. There was a whirring sound, a humming and buzzing. Tiny creatures with wings and claws, stings and beaks flew around Ishtar. Poking, pricking, biting, eating, gnawing, devouring, they contaminated Ishtar with diseases. Eye diseases, foot diseases, heart diseases, head diseases, arm diseases, mouth diseases. Until Ishtar's body was pierced with holes, punctured with wounds, covered with sores. Until Ishtar could no longer see, hear, speak, feel, think, cry out. Until she became a piece of rotting meat, a lifeless corpse.

'Hang her from the hook on the wall,' cried Ereshkigal.

The rotting corpse of Ishtar was hung from a rusty hook. Then Ereshkigal sat on her throne, alone in the dark, her head bowed in misery. Darkness covered the Great Below.

Three days passed and Ishtar had not come back from the Land of the Dead. Everyone wept and the funeral rite was performed for the Goddess of Love and War. Darkness covered the Great Above. There was no morning star or evening star. The world went awry. No bulls mounted cows. Lovers slept alone. Girls stayed at home and did not go out. Wives slept with their grandmothers. Husbands drank too much and slept in the street.

Anu, God of the Sky, looked down to earth, saw the disturbance and understood that Ishtar had left the world. The world could not survive without her, the Goddess of Love and War must be brought back. Anu created a man, a strapping lad made for pure arousal. Anu wrapped a loin cloth around his strong thighs, decorated his bronzed neck with jewels, hung a fine cloak over his broad shoulders and named him Mr Good-Looks. Then Anu gave him a water skin, filled not with earthly water but heavenly water, the Water of Life. Then Anu instructed Mr Good-Looks and sent him down to the Great Below.

Mr Good-Looks strode across earth. He was very handsome, though no one admired him because they were all asleep. Good-Looks walked down into the darkness, all the way to the entrance of the underworld. Good-Looks called for the gatekeeper, and Neti said that he too must follow the ancient rites. Mr Good-Looks was made to leave his water skin outside the gates. And then at each gate he removed: sandals; cloak pin; cloak; necklace; belt; robe and loin cloth.

Mr Good-Looks entered the underworld naked. His body gleamed, lighting up the darkness. Ereshkigal lifted her head, blinked and stared. Mr Good-Looks bowed, took Ereshkigal's hand and kissed it. 'My Queen, I have heard so much about you!'

A smile flickered across Ereshkigal's lips and she climbed down from her throne. 'Bring a couch,' she called.

A golden couch was brought and they lay down together. And the lad got to work. It was what he was made for. Mr Good-Looks took the Queen of the Dead in his arms and embraced her. Ereshkigal relaxed. Good-Looks kissed her fingertips, her wrists, the backs of her arms. Ereshkigal softened. Good-Looks kissed the crease of her neck, the roundest part of her cheeks, the side of her lips. Ereshkigal melted. Good-Looks kissed her mouth. Ereshkigal was aroused, 'You cannot imagine how lonely it is down here,' she sighed. 'With only ghosts for company. Mr Good-Looks, you please me. Let me give you a gift. What will you have? Take something, anything. What would you like?'

'I don't need anything,' said Good-Looks, 'except you.'

And he kissed Ereshkigal on her breast. Then he lingered over her nipple, and said, 'A drink from my water skin would be nice.'

'Is that all,' moaned Ereshkigal, and she called out, 'Bring the skin!'

The water skin was brought through the seven gates. Mr Good-Looks took the skin, pressed it to his lips and filled his mouth. Then he turned, and spat the water out onto the lump of meat hanging from the hook on the wall. The Water of Life splashed across the rotting corpse of Ishtar. The flesh quivered, the wounds disappeared, the sores mended, the flesh healed. The diseases vanished. Ishtar breathed in, opened her eyes and came back to life. She was healed and whole and stood before her sister.

Ereshkigal leapt to her feet, furious, 'How stupid I am!'

She bit her knuckles, struck her thigh.

'You tricked me! Curse you Good-Looks! Curse you forever. Curse you to eat rubbish from the streets and drink from the city drains. Curse you to live in a small patch of shade by the city wall where everyone who passes by will spit on you.'

But Ereshkigal could not curse Ishtar.

'You have been given life again and I cannot take it away. But if you want Tammuz, you must pay for him. And the payment is this, Tammuz must visit me once a year. I will call him down and he will be mine. The rest of the time he is yours.'

A faint shadow appeared, it was Tammuz and Ishtar took his ghostly hand. As they walked through each gate, Tammuz regained his form and became young and strong again. And at each gate Neti returned Ishtar's robes, jewels, crown, weapons. As they followed the path of ashes upwards, rain fell, grass became green, flowers opened and the world awoke. Ishtar and Tammuz returned from the Great Below. Tammuz was washed and dressed in red robes, lapis lazuli pipes were played, girls danced. A golden bed was made and Ishtar and Tammuz lay down together at last.

As for Mr Good-Looks, he sat in a small patch of shade by the city gates, but no one spat on him, he did not eat rubbish, or drink from drains because a woman passed by.

'Hey, haven't I seen you somewhere before? I've just been making some food, why don't you come home and join me?' The woman took Mr Good-Looks home, gave him whatever he wanted and he gave her whatever she wanted! And so Mr Good-Looks sat by the city gates each day, but never for long.

Each year, after the harvest, Ereshkigal calls Tammuz down to the underworld. She is no longer lonely, at last she has someone to keep her company. But when Tammuz descends, the world weeps for the loss of the God of Spring. The ground becomes parched and dry and nothing grows. Everyone weeps so Tammuz will return. Ishtar makes her eternal journey to wake him and bring him back. Then grief is over, desire is satisfied and love fills everyone.

Ishtar, mighty, majestic, radiant,
brightest star in the heaven,
torch of the earth,
you fill the sky with light.
We have cleaned the house.
We have tidied the garden.
Bring us wealth, give us health.
Ishtar protect us, so Tammuz will ripen our grain.

The story of Ishtar and Tammuz was written in cuneiform on tablets of clay around the seventh century BC. Fragments of many versions exist that take different paths through the narrative, some with side-stories and backstories that have distinct outcomes and various endings. In the earlier Sumerian version – 'The descent of Innana' – Tammuz is called Dumuzi.

I like the later Babylonian version, partly because of its humour, and also because Tammuz is still the name for the month of June in many parts of the Middle East today. In Ancient Mesopotamia crops were harvested in June and the festival of Tammuz was celebrated. The women of the city wept for Tammuz, lost God of Spring, and laments were sung. The king impersonated Tammuz and the priestess became Ishtar. The king visited Ishtar to enact the sacred marriage rite so that the land would be fertile again.

A green garnet Mesopotamian seal from about 1000 BC shows the Goddess Ishtar being honoured by a king, above her is an image of the planet Venus. Ishtar was the original Venus, and in cuneiform was represented by an eight-pointed star. The myth could have been a cosmic enactment of the movement of the planets and stars. This myth is the oldest written version of a story that follows a pattern repeated by so many other myths, including the myths of Isis and Osiris, Demeter and Persephone, Venus and Adonis, Christ and Mary.

The Net of Venus

Roman

Venus, Goddess of Beauty, was dressed by two veiled maidens, the Horai, the Hours. Beauty was dressed by Time. They wrapped the finest slip around her curvy body, placed a wreath of gold on her head, hung jewels from her ears and a thread of silver round her neck. Then they tied a fine band of pearls across her body. The girdle of pearls wound between her breasts and beneath her heart. The girdle had magical properties, no one could resist its spell, all would be drawn to Venus. So wherever Venus went she spread desire. All the gods fell in love with Venus and among her lovers were Neptune, Bacchus, Pluto and Jupiter himself.

Jupiter became concerned and declared that Venus should be restrained. He arranged a marriage between Venus and Vulcan, God of Fire. The marriage seemed to be Jupiter's joke, the most beautiful goddess marrying the most unattractive god. Vulcan was a hulk of a man who spent all his time working in his forge. He was covered in grime, always sweaty, his back hunched, his limbs twisted from hard labour. Venus was not impressed. And as soon as the wedding was over she tightened her girdle and Mars, God of War, caught her eye.

When Vulcan was working in his forge, Venus led Mars to her chamber and enjoyed him. And after that she enjoyed him every afternoon! One time, as they lay entwined on Venus's bed, the sun beamed through an upper window and lit up their passionate embrace. The sun was horrified. What outrageous deception, and from a new bride! The sun rushed to tell Vulcan. When Vulcan heard that his wife was having an affair, he was so shocked he dropped the sword he was crafting and it shattered on the ground.

'My heart is shattered too,' said Vulcan. 'I will destroy them.'

Vulcan took up his tools and began to work on something new. With tiny taps he forged a net, crafted of bronze so fine the links could not be seen. The net was lighter than a spider's web and reacted to the slightest touch, closing tight in an instant. The net was a love trap. Vulcan arranged the net above Venus's bed, hanging it from the wooden beams in the ceiling.

That afternoon, as Venus pulled Mars onto the bed and drew him inside her, they triggered the net. It fell on top of them, its tiny links clamping tight, fastening around their bodies, locking in place and they were unable to move. Vulcan threw open the doors and roared, 'Come and see what I have caught! Come and see the guilty ones.'

Gods and goddesses crowded around the bedroom door and saw Mars and Venus ensnared. Their bodies were trapped in the gleaming net. Venus and Mars were caught fast in the very act of love.

'Look!' cried Vulcan. 'See their shameful behaviour!'

The gods and goddesses roared with laughter. And Mercury turned to Apollo and said, 'I wish I could get shamed like that!'

The gods begged Vulcan to set Mars and Venus free. But Vulcan refused. So Bacchus slipped off and fetched his wine jug and bowl. He poured out dark liquid, and against his own rules, gave Vulcan four bowls of wine. Vulcan started showing off, boasting about his skills, then displaying how his love trap worked. Mars and Venus were released at last.

Venus did not apologise to Vulcan. Instead she vowed to herself that she would never be faithful. She would cast her net and spread it wide! And she murmured, 'I will punish the sun for this. I'll make him suffer for love.'

Venus made the sun fall in love with a simple peasant girl. The sun followed the girl everywhere, even to her grave. His beloved was buried alive and the sun kept watch, pushing his hot rays into the cold soil to bring her back to life. And the sun is still trying to keep his beloved warm.

Meanwhile, Mercury swaggered up to Venus and set about getting himself shamed as soon as possible! Venus tightened her girdle, he would be the first of many.

Venus and Aphrodite share the same stories. I wanted to include Venus because her image lived on through sculptures, paintings and poems long after the Roman Empire was over.

Freyja, Goddess of Sex

Scandinavia

Freyja, Goddess of Sex, lived in Sessrúmnir. Her hall was impenetrable from the outside. The doors, walls and windows had no fixed place and only Freyja knew the spell that could open them. Freyja lived alone with her cats. The cats had eyes that glowed and tufted ears. They carried the long train of Freyja's gown or pulled her chariot. Sometimes Freyja would put on her falcon suit, a skin of feathers, become a falcon and fly around the world in disguise. The Goddess of Sex enchanted everyone. Gods, giants, spirits, dwarfs all wanted her. The great God Odin thought she belonged to him. But Freyja was married to Odr.

One day Odr went for a walk and never came back. No one knew what happened to him. Freyja wept golden tears of grief at all the things she would never do with her beloved Odr, at all the things she would miss sharing with him. When the tears were dry Freyja promised herself to herself, she would never belong to anyone and set about a life of satisfying her own desire. Sometimes Freyja is known as Frigg. And she gave the word frigg to women, a word for the act of female pleasure, of female fulfilment. Among Freyja's lovers were Frey, her own brother; Ottar, who she rode in the form of a golden boar; and Odin. Everywhere she went she spread desire.

One evening, Freyja was racing home with her cats through the mountains when she saw a light glinting from a cleft in a rock. She called to the cats and the chariot came to a stop. Freyja peeped through the crack and saw a cave illuminated by a fire and four dwarfs hunched over an anvil. They were working with tiny hammers and tongs, tapping and shaping, forging a necklace. The necklace seemed to wink at Freyja. The goddess uttered a spell, the cleft opened and she pushed between the rocks into the cave. She leaned over the anvil. The necklace was made of fine golden spirals linked together, one inside another, whorls within whorls. The necklace looked like interlocking planets, like the universe turning.

'That is a thing of beauty,' she said.

The dwarfs kept working. 'It is the Necklace of the Brisings. Our necklace. We are the Brisings.'

'How much is it?' asked Freyja.

'It is not for sale.'

'I can give you silver, gold, diamonds. How much do you want?'

'The Brisings live underground, we have jewels without end!' laughed the dwarfs.

'What don't you have?' asked the goddess.

The dwarfs stopped working and looked at Freyja. 'Sex!' they said. 'We want you.'

Freyja was repulsed. The dwarves were covered in thick hair, they had bulbous noses, bulging eyes, gnarled fingers. Time had not improved their appearance and they were still as unattractive as their ancestors, the wriggling maggots! Freyja did not feel a cat's whisker of desire. But the necklace began to move, its spirals started to whirr, the whorls hummed and buzzed, vibrating with the harmony of the spheres. The necklace was alive and spoke to Freyja. It was worth anything. Everything.

'I must have it,' she said. Freyja held out her hand to the dwarfs and they bowed.

'Alfrigg.'

'Dvalin.'

'Berling.'

'Grerr.'

The Brisings led the Goddess of Sex into their underground cavern. And Freyja spent four long nights there. The mountain echoed with the dwarfs delight. And then on the morning of the fifth day, the dwarves clasped the Necklace of the Brisings around Freyja's neck. The links and chains shifted and moved to fit the curves of her neck. The whorls began to hum, and golden power vibrated through her skin, her veins and into her bones. Freyja sighed, it had been worth it.

The cats carried her back to Sessrúmnir. The goddess ate, took off her robes, bathed and climbed into bed naked, wearing nothing but her precious necklace. After she had honoured her name and satisfied herself, she fell into a deep, healing sleep.

There was a buzz and a tiny fly penetrated the impenetrable Sessrúmnir. It was Loki, Trickster God. He could change his shape into anything he wanted. He had searched the walls of Sessrúmnir and found a thin crack. Loki became a fly and flew through the crack. He buzzed over the sleeping cats, who twitched their ears and tails. One lifted a claw but Loki whizzed past. He was looking for the necklace, he'd been sent by Odin to fetch it. He flew into Freyja's chamber and saw the glorious shape of her body stretched out across the bed and around her neck the living necklace. The clasp was beneath her neck. So Loki turned into a flea and wondered which part of Freyja he should bite! He crawled across the mound of her belly, the arch of her waist, to her breasts and dug his tiny jaws into her sweet flesh. Freyja scratched her skin in her sleep and rolled over onto her side. Loki silently turned back into himself and unclasped the necklace. Sessrúmnir might be impenetrable from the outside, but Loki swiftly unlocked the main door from the inside and slipped away into the night.

Freyja woke to a cold wind blowing through her hall. She put her fingers to her throat and the necklace was gone.

'Thief! Thief!' she cried.

Freyja called the cats, leapt into her chariot and raced off. 'There is only one capable of this.'

She urged the cats over Bifrost, the rainbow bridge, to Asgard and into Odin's chamber.

Odin was sitting on his throne, his two spying ravens, Hugin and Mugin, Thought and Memory, perched on his shoulders. In his hands was the necklace.

'That belongs to me!' roared Freyja.

'How could you have sex with those disgusting creatures?' said Odin.

'So, that's it?' said Freyja. 'You're jealous.'

Odin turned the necklace in his fingers. 'I thought you were mine,' he said.

'I belong to nobody. And I paid for that necklace. Do I have to pay for it all over again?'

'Spread war and misery instead of desire and sex, then you may have it.'

'Only hatred will satisfy you? Then hatred you will have. But you will never have me again. Give me the necklace.'

'My ravens will be watching,' said Odin and placed the necklace in her hands.

Freyja put the Necklace of the Brisings around her neck. It shivered with pleasure to be home, filling her with power. Then, wearing her falcon suit, she led the Valkyries to war. She flew over battlefields with her sisters: Skuld – shield carrier; Gunnr – war; Hlökk – noise; Skeggjöld – axeage; Göll – tumult; Hildr – battle; Skögul – shaker; and Gondul – spear hurler. Before battle they would rub their menstrual blood on their warriors lips and cheeks to give them courage. During battle they would become falcons, ravens, crows and fly over the warriors screeching, urging them to carnage. After battle, Freyja and the Valkyries would walk through the ranks of the fallen wearing bloodstained dresses and helmets. The Valkyries would carry the heroes to Valhalla, the halls of the slain. Freyja would choose the bravest dead, wash them in the Spring of Life and take them to Sessrúmnir. She would welcome them into her own hall with wine and food and give them an afterlife of pure pleasure.

Odin's ravens watched. Freyja kept her promise, spreading war and misery. But she was the Goddess of Sex and when she put on her precious necklace nothing, not ravens nor Odin himself, could stop her spreading desire.

Chang'e, Lady of the Moon

China

Chang'e longed to be in the arms of her husband, archer Yi. But Yi was too busy. Chang'e was always waiting for him. Yi was too busy being a warrior, then a farmer, then he was on another planet.

Warrior Yi loosed arrows and shot nine of the ten Sun Crows. The divine archer saved the world from burning up. Afterwards Chang'e took Yi to bed. She embraced him tightly, her lover had returned, at last he was beside her! The whole world was grateful to warrior Yi. And the Queen Mother of the West, Xi Wang Mu, gave Yi a reward. She presented him with a tiny pink pill.

'This pill will give you eternal life,' said the Queen Mother. 'It has been pounded from my peaches of immortality. But you need to be purified in order to take it. Before you can become immortal you must fast for a whole year.'

Yi hid the pill in the wooden beams of his roof. For the next year he did not eat. He existed on the perfume of flowers and spent his time working hard in the fields. Yi became a farmer, tilling the soil and planting seeds. And Chang'e waited, again.

One day, Chang'e saw a tiny light glowing from the beams of the roof. She climbed into the attic and saw the light was emanating from something that looked like a little pink sweet. Chang'e lifted the sweet to her lips, it smelled of ripe peaches. She popped it into her mouth and it tasted of perfume. Her face suddenly felt hot, her fingers shone and her whole body began to glow. Then her feet lifted from the ground. Chang'e floated up into the air. Her body was as light as a feather, and she drifted out of a window and across the fields.

Down below she saw farmer Yi digging the soil. 'Help! Help!' she cried as she floated above him. Her husband ran after her. He leapt into the air and grabbed the end of her robe. But he could not hold onto her, Chang'e was so light the wind caught her and she blew away. She soared up through the blue sky, through the clouds, through the stars and landed with a bump on the moon.

It was cold and hard up there. And Chang'e felt utterly alone. There was no point waiting for Yi anymore, he was on another planet. She sobbed and sobbed. When at last she stopped crying, she heard a pounding sound. Chang'e floated across the rocky surface of the moon and came to a single tree. Beneath the tree was a hare pounding pink paste in a pestle and mortar. The hare was one of the Queen Mother's faithful servants. The hare was pounding Xi Wang Mu's magic peaches, extracting the elixir of life and making it into the pills of immortality. Chang'e sat down beneath the tree. Her glowing beauty covered the moon. She became the Lady of the Moon, and she shone down on earth and filled her husband's face with silver light. Yi looked up at his wife, and for the first time he was filled with longing. He stared up at the moon and Chang'e looked down on him. They were both filled with sadness, with impossible yearning.

The Queen Mother felt sorry for them. And so once a month, when the moon is full, she transports Yi to his beloved. Then Chang'e holds her husband in her arms again. And full moon parties are held down on earth to celebrate the Lady of the Moon and her lover. There is dressing up, cosmic dances, moon cakes, magical rituals, white rabbits, lots of wine and human beings fall in love! And when the moon is full, you can look at its glowing face and see the hare bent over the pestle and mortar pounding the pills of immortality, but you will never be able to eat one.

As Chang'e waits for the full moon each month, she watches over earth. She creates the pull of the tides, the seasons of rain and women's cycles. As Chang'e waxes and wanes, as she moves from light to dark to light once more, she reminds us that life returns and returns; that, like the moon, immortality does exist, life comes again and again.

Aphrodite and Anchises

Greece

Aphrodite was thinking of all her love affairs. There was Hermes, Ares, Poseidon, Dionysus, Zeus and more. She laughed at all the liaisons gone wrong, the broken hearts! Zeus watched her.

'How cruel,' he said.

'A god may have his way with anything he desires, but it's cruel if a goddess does the same?' said Aphrodite. 'Gods can make love with beasts and mortals and father their children, but goddesses may not? I make love to whoever I like and I will mother their children too.'

Zeus parted the clouds that swirled around Mount Olympus and looked down on earth. He pointed at the island of Crete, 'Then take him!'

Aphrodite looked down at a young herdsman following his cattle. Anchises was a simple lad living in a tent on top of Mount Ida.

'Do you want a war?' she said. 'Then I will enjoy him, and have his child. I will mother a boy who will change history.'

Aphrodite flashed down to Crete, to her temple at Paphos. There, the Three Graces bathed her. They rubbed perfumed oil into her skin and hair and dressed her in an airy robe. Aphrodite walked through the fields and forests to the top of Mount Ida. As she walked, wild animals followed her, grey wolves waving their tails, lions bowing their heads, leopards rubbing against her bare legs, gazelles nuzzling their noses into her hand and birds circling above her head. She saw the herdsman's tent in the distance and Anchises sitting under the canopy playing a lute. Aphrodite lifted her hand towards the wild beasts and raised a finger, filling them with such desire that they all ran off to couple. Then Aphrodite wrapped her goddess glory in a secret cloud and made her way to the tent disguised as a mortal girl.

Anchises looked up, 'Where have you come from? Are you a spirit of nature? Or a goddess from the sky?'

'I am a mere mortal. And I'm looking for Anchises. I was a maiden at the Temple of Artemis serving the great goddess, when the messenger Hermes caught me and carried me here. He placed me on this mountain and told me I am to be the bride of Anchises.'

The herdsman's heart thumped in his chest, all his dreams and prayers had come true in a moment. 'I am he. I am Anchises.'

He invited the maiden into his tent. He made her a seat on a pile of soft hides and furs, and gave her cool creamy milk to drink.

'Shall we go and meet your family as tradition requires?' he asked.

'Surely we are allowed to get to know each other first?' said Aphrodite, winding her fingers through his hand, 'if we are to be husband and wife?'

A smile flickered on her lips as she loosened her robe. Heavy perfume filled the air and Anchises was unable to resist. He pulled her into his arms and they fell on the furs. Like wolves, leopards, gazelles, they took their pleasure from each other again and again, until they lay exhausted. Then Aphrodite unbound the cloud, rose into the air above Anchises and revealed her goddess glory. Golden Aphrodite filled the tent with light so bright Anchises was forced to shield his eyes from her divine beauty.

'Have mercy Goddess!' he cried. 'If I had known who you were I would never have touched you. A mortal must not make love with a god and now bad luck will follow me forever.'

'I have conceived,' said Aphrodite, 'and it cannot be undone. But your son will be brought up in secret and no one will know what happened here today. Have no fear, your son is destined for great things.'

Aphrodite returned to Zeus triumphant. She had seduced a mortal and would give birth to a mortal boy. When the baby was born she called him Aeneas and gave him to the forest nymphs to bring up in secret. No one knew who the boy's parents were. Except for Anchises, who watched his son Aeneas become a powerful warrior, then leader of the Trojan army. Aeneas would change history.

Anchises could not help feeling proud of his son. And one night after much drinking, he boasted that he was the warrior's father, bragging that he had made love with the Golden One herself! Suddenly, there was a crack of thunder. Zeus sent a bolt of lightning that struck Anchises on the leg, maiming him forever. Anchises had met his bad luck and limped for the rest of his life. When the city of Troy burned, Anchises could not run and was unable to escape from the flames. But Aphrodite was watching and she sent Aeneas to help. The warrior lifted his father up onto his back and carried him through the fire to safety. Aphrodite smiled as the city sank into ruins, she had got her war.

It was Aphrodite who was partly responsible for the Trojan War. She bribed Paris to her give her the golden apple 'for the fairest', in exchange for Helen, the most beautiful woman in the world. Helen's abduction caused the war between the Greeks and Trojans. Aphrodite's stories merge with those of Venus, and for the myth of how Aphrodite really fell in love, see the Roman 'Venus and Adonis'.

Isis and Osiris

Egypt

Isis, Mistress of Magic, Speaker of Spells, took her own brother Osiris as her lover, husband, king. When their hands touched green shoots appeared. When their lips met buds opened. When their bodies merged the ground became fertile. Their desire made everything grow. Together they ruled. Isis, with a crown like a throne, taught humans magic, spells to heal, protect, destroy. Osiris, with a flail for threshing in one hand, taught the arts of irrigation and cultivation, how to sow barley, grow wheat and harvest grain. And with a crook for shepherding in the other hand, Osiris taught the taming and husbandry of animals. Their sister Nepthys, with a headdress like a house, became Goddess of the Hearth. The Lady of the House taught bread-making, fire-lighting, cookery and the arts of making a home. Their brother Set was a warrior, God of Storms. In one hand he carried a curved scimitar, in the other, a spear. Set shifted the sky with his weapons, producing rain with a strike, whipping up waves, summoning and banishing clouds. Under the protection of the four gods earth flourished.

The God of Storms watched his siblings and was filled with bitter jealousy. They had palaces and gardens while he only had mountain tops and dark skies. Set planned to take the throne. He organised a feast in honour of Osiris. Only men were invited, and as the guests arrived fine chains were placed around their necks and perfume pressed into their hair. There was drinking, feasting and a bard praising Osiris.

Then Set announced, 'A game!' He revealed a long, low, painted box, decorated with flowers and engraved with gold.

'Whoever fits inside this box can have it!' said Set.

One by one, guests took off their sandals and stepped into the box. They were too short, too tall, too thin, too fat, no one fitted the box.

'Try, my brother,' said Set.

Osiris took off his crown and slippers. He stepped into the box. His feet just brushed the bottom, his head just touched the top. He fitted the box perfectly.

'It was made to measure!' cried Set, slamming a painted lid on top of the box. Warriors rushed forward and hammered nails into the lid and poured molten lead around the rim. The box was sealed and inside Osiris suffocated and died. The box had become a coffin.

Set placed Osiris's crown on his head and ordered the coffin to be thrown into the River Nile. The box was hurled into the river but it did not sink. The box floated away, carried downstream, pulled by the tides out to sea. The coffin had become a boat.

Isis was stricken with grief. She shaved off half her hair and ripped her dress as all widows did, following the ancient Egyptian custom of mourning. She knotted her red sash around her waist, then, weeping and wailing, set off along the River Nile looking for the box. She uttered lamentations for her lover and they were heard throughout the land. She passed a group of children playing on the shore and asked if they had seen anything floating on the water. The children nodded and pointed, they had seen a box glittering in the sunlight. It had drifted past and floated out to sea. Isis followed the river, among tall reed beds, through deep marshes until the river became wider and spilled into the open sea.

The box bobbed on the waves, sailing through the night and was washed up on the shores of the kingdom of Byblos. In the pitch dark a root pushed out of the box. The root dug down into the sandy beach. Green shoots curled from the box and leaves sprouted. A trunk grew, thick and tall, rising up in the darkness completely enclosing the box. When dawn broke, a huge spreading tree stood on the beach. The boat had become a tree.

The citizens of Byblos gathered on the beach to gaze at the miraculous tree. News spread and the Queen of Byblos came to admire the tree that had risen in the darkness.

'This tree has power. It will be the central pillar in my Great Hall,' commanded the Queen.

The tree was cut down, carried to the palace and heaved into place. The tree had become a pillar.

The story of the tree that had grown overnight reached Isis. She knew at once that only her lover could make a tree grow in the dark. And she set sail for Byblos. When she reached the kingdom, Isis twisted her red sash and turned into an old woman. She sat by the city well, plaiting women's hair in the latest Egyptian fashions, then breathing on them, infusing their skin with musk and sandalwood. The Queen of Byblos requested the old woman's talents in the palace. And Isis became the Queen's own serving maid, dressing the Queen, arranging her hair and helping with her newborn baby boy. When the baby cried, Isis put her finger in the baby's mouth. Milk and honey flowed from her finger and the boy stopped crying.

One night the Queen woke to the smell of smoke. The Queen followed the smell to the Great Hall. Flying round the central pillar was a swallow, circling the massive tree trunk, tapping its beak on the wood. Beneath the tree was a fire and lying in the flames was the baby prince. The Queen screamed and snatched the baby from the fire, but the baby gurgled and smiled. The Queen turned him over in her arms, examining his body and there was not a single burn on his flesh. The baby was unharmed. The swallow fluttered to the ground and there stood the Goddess Isis with her arms outstretched.

'Foolish Queen!' uttered the goddess. 'I was not burning your son, I was burning his mortality, burning up his death. If you had left him in the fire he would have become a god and lived forever. Now he will be mortal and die like all human beings.'

The Queen fell to her knees, 'Forgive me, great Goddess. Take something. Anything.'

'I want the tree,' said Isis. 'And a boat.'

The Queen bowed. Isis lifted the tree from the stone floor as if she was plucking a flower. She broke the trunk open as if she was breaking bread. And inside was the box, the painted flowers and patterns of gold unspoiled. The pillar had become a box. The Queen of Byblos built a temple to hold the remains of the precious tree. Its wood was wrapped in linen and preserved for future generations to kneel before and be blessed by. But the painted box was carried to a boat and Isis set sail for Egypt. Far out to sea Isis prised away the lead and levered open the box. Lying inside was Osiris, looking just as if he was asleep. The box had become a coffin.

Isis sailed down the River Nile, then followed a narrow tributary through waving papyrus reeds to a small hut standing on stilts above the water. She dragged the box up wooden steps into the hut. She removed the lid, lit a lamp and placed it at Osiris's head. Isis kissed his face and wept.

'My lover, my husband, my king I know the secret name of Ra, I can bring back the dead. But the spell is powerful and I need our sister's help. Nepthys is the light to my dark, the morning star to my evening star. I will fetch her and together we will bring you back to life.' And Isis left Osiris hidden in the reeds and sailed to her sister.

That night it was a full moon, perfect for hunting. The God of Storms stocked his skiff with harpoon, nets, retriever cats and went hunting. He sailed through shallow waters, the cats sitting in the prow of the boat catching fish with their claws. Set saw a light shimmering through the reeds. He was curious and followed the light to the hut on stilts. Set found the painted box illuminated in the lamplight, its lid open with Osiris lying inside. Murderous rage filled Set, he drew his scimitar and slashed the body. He sliced through skin, flesh, sinew, bone, chopping Osiris into fourteen pieces. Set piled the pieces into his boat and sailed down the Nile, throwing pieces of the body into the river. All the pieces sank under the waves and Set cried, 'No one will take the crown from me!'

When Isis and Nepthys returned they found the box empty. The Mistress of Magic twisted her red sash and uttered a spell. Feathers pushed out of the sisters' arms, their faces became beaks, their feet claws. The sisters turned into birds. Two kites spread their wings and flew over the Nile looking for their brother. They scoured the river with sharp eyes, and when they saw a piece of Osiris's body they dived down, caught it in their talons and carried it back to the hut. For each piece they found, the sisters conjured up a stone statue of Osiris on the river bank, to trick Set into believing the body part had been buried beneath a memorial. And this is why there are so many statues of Osiris along the banks of the River Nile.

The sisters found thirteen pieces of the body. But could not find the fourteenth piece. It had sunk down through the water into the thick mud at the bottom of the river and had been eaten by the lepidotus, a fish later cursed by the Egyptians, and which became extinct. Inside the hut, the sisters wrapped each piece of Osiris's body in linen imbued with pine resin and frankincense. They placed the linen-wrapped pieces in the box, head, arms, hands, chest, spine, abdomen, hips, legs and feet. But the fourteenth piece, Osiris's phallus was missing. Isis took a dry stick and placed it in Osiris's groin.

'Let us lift up his head again. Let us re-join his bones. Let us raise his loins. Let us bring our beloved, our brother back.'

Isis and Nepthys stood over the body and spread their wings, the tips of their feathers touching, protecting the body. The sisters fluttered their feathers and wind blew from their wings. A sweet wind. The sisters chanted:

> Like ears of corn gathered into one sheaf,
> limbs gather together into one body.
> Like the Nile swelling into flood,
> fluid increase, heart pump, blood flow.
> Wheat grow again.
> Dark moon return.
> Sun rise again.
> Isis has your hand.
> Nepthys has your foot.
> Osiris awaken,
> Osiris rise up.
> Live, Osiris!

The sisters beat their wings faster and faster and gave life to the body. Bone and flesh began to mend. Veins joined, heart pumped, blood flowed. Then Isis knelt and pressed her heart to Osiris's heart and uttered the secret magic name of Ra. Breath came, breath rose, breath filled the body and Osiris sat up. Lovers and siblings embraced. And Osiris spoke, 'This magic will only last one night on earth. But it will last forever in the underworld. At dawn I will die again and be reborn Lord of the Underworld.'

The God of Harvest produced a feast and they celebrated. Isis had one last night with her lover, hands, lips, bodies met and the dry stick burst into blossom. Osiris left a seed inside Isis. A seed that would become their son Horus. Isis would pass the secret name of Ra from her heart to her son's heart, just as she had promised. And later Horus would avenge his father's death and take the crown from Set. Just before dawn the sisters bid goodbye to their brother. And Osiris was reborn, Lord of the Underworld. With his crook in one hand and his flail in the other, Osiris became the shepherd and harvester of souls.

Osiris is portrayed in papyrus manuscripts with a green face, like the earth that turns green when the Nile floods. The Lord of the Underworld was the first to be wrapped in linen and mummified and all Egyptians followed after him, wrapped in linen and preserved with juniper, cinnamon and pine resin, their painted coffins decorated with images of Isis, her wings outspread across their hearts. In this coffin boat the soul made its journey to the underworld to meet Osiris and face the final test.

Osiris took the heart of each soul and weighed it on the scales of truth. The heart was weighed against the feather of justice, the feather of Maat, to see which was lighter, heart or feather? If the heart was lighter than the feather it could be reborn, set free to enter paradise, the Field of Reeds. But if the heart was heavier than the feather it was devoured by the monster Ammit, Eater of the Dead.

How can a heart ever be lighter than a feather? How? Through love. Love makes all hearts lighter than feathers.

Erzulie Freda

Vodou, Haiti

If you want the help of Erzulie Freda, hang up a wedding dress – blue lace is her favourite. Spread out a veil. Leave her a powder puff and the latest lipstick. Serve pink champagne in an ice cold glass. Leave her a cake as light as air on an antique plate. Flambé bananas in butter, add sugar and rum and the aroma will call her. Offer her jewels, crystal earrings, a glittering necklace. Light a rose-scented candle, burn fine incense. Everything must be the best – no cheap gifts for the Goddess of Love!

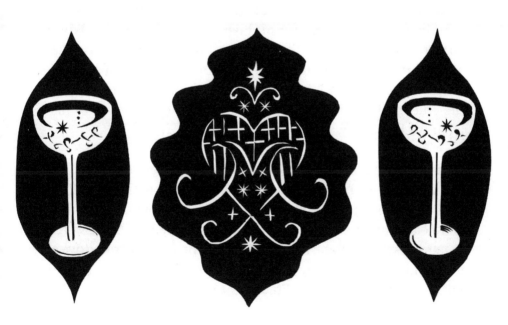

Erzulie Freda adores beauty and luxury. She will array herself in the dress and jewels. She will tease and flirt. She will teach you how to succeed in attracting what you desire. But as soon as the Goddess of Love is alone she wraps her arms around her knees and sits huddled, weeping in her wedding dress. She weeps without stopping, for love that never lasts, weeps for love that always passes.

Erzulie Freda wears three wedding rings, one for each of her husbands. Her first husband was Damballah, the great Sky God, a white serpent who created the stars and planets from his seven thousand coils and set the earth spinning. Her second husband was Agwe, God of the Sea, patron to ships and sailors. Her third husband was Ogun, God of Fire, a flaming warrior. What became of her husbands? No one knows. No one found out. No one told her. But each one disappeared. They were too busy creating, sailing, fighting. They went to work and never came back. They had affairs, or married others. They were lost at sea and drowned. They were captured and tortured. They were wounded and died alone on the battlefield. They were taken as slaves, then murdered in the street. Erzulie Freda weeps for them all. Erzulie weeps for us all, for all lovers, all husbands and wives, all parents and children. She weeps for all who have been taken away, torn asunder. Erzulie weeps for the sweetness of love, the shortness of love, for love that never lasts long. Erzulie weeps at the cruelty of death, that death is always so close, ready to take what we love away.

Lavish the Goddess of Love with gifts, serve her, adore her and she will help you. Draw her veve on the floor with white flour, chalk, cornmeal; this will call her, bring her down. Her symbol is a heart entwined with flowers and scattered with stars. This is her talisman. Chant to her, 'Goddess of Love, attract love to me, call love to me, bring love to me. Erzulie Freda give me flow, make my life flow. Erzulie Freda protect me.'

Erzulie Freda is part of the family of Vodou Loa spirits. There are many Erzulies, each with a different quality and power, from passionate to angry, mothering to vengeful, and there are different rituals to invoke each and gain their specific blessings. Vodou has its roots in deities from West African religions, the Yoruba, Kongo and Fon peoples in particular. These ancient traditions were brought by enslaved Africans to the Caribbean, where they merged with Roman Catholic iconography and rituals.

Venus and Adonis

Roman

Venus had many affairs but never fell in love herself. And she had many children. Some were born in secret, some were given to nymphs to raise, some had no idea who their father was, others did not know Venus was their mother. Among her children were Hermaphroditus, son of Mercury, who merged with a lover, becoming neither male nor female but both, and Priapus, son of Bacchus, who was born with such an enormous phallus Venus hid him in the mountains. Venus had daughters too, Fortuna, Goddess of Fate and Suadela, Goddess of Persuasion. But Venus was a lover not a mother, and she sent all her children away.

All except one. No one knew who his father was. Perhaps he was the only son of Vulcan? Or was his father Zephyrus the wind? Maybe it was Mars, or was it Jupiter? No one was sure. But the baby was gorgeous with golden curls, rosy lips, chubby cheeks, dimples and rolls of fat around his thighs. Venus adored him and called him Cupid. Love. The Goddess of Desire had given birth to Love.

Venus indulged Cupid and encouraged his naughtiness. She got Vulcan to make him a tiny bow and set of arrows. Then she urged Cupid to mischief, sending him across the world on her missions to burn up hearts, ignite old flames, destroy homes. Cupid's aim was true and his love dart always hit its mark. No one could escape Cupid's arrow. Not even his own mother.

One day Venus was parting the clouds on top of Mount Olympus and looking down on earth to see what was going on, when her son crept up behind her. Cupid, with his quiver of arrows slung over one shoulder, bent to press his rosy lips to his mother's cheek, when one of his arrows grazed her neck. At that very moment Venus saw a young man. Her heart leapt. The youth was hunting, his sturdy arms carrying a bow, his powerful legs bronzed by the sun. It was Adonis, the hunter. Cupid's magic arrow enflamed Venus and she was overwhelmed with desire for Adonis.

Venus flashed down to earth. Adonis was cleaning his weapons and did not look up. This was not the reaction the goddess was used to. She tightened her girdle of pearls, it never failed. But Adonis picked up his weapons and ran off to hunt. Venus tucked her robe above her knees and ran after him. She chased Adonis as he hunted stag, fox, hare. When Adonis stretched out under the shade of an olive tree to rest, Venus lay beside him. Adonis did not move to kiss her, he did not even take her hand. Venus suddenly felt shy, unable to reach out, unable to seduce him.

'Cupid have mercy,' she murmured. 'What has happened?' This was not her usual lust but something quite different, something she had never felt before. Venus had fallen in love.

The goddess could not bear to be without Adonis. She neglected her rites, no longer visited her temples, did not attend the assembly of the gods. Instead, she followed Adonis everywhere. He seemed to accept her, and when he was resting, Venus would wrap her arms around him and cling to him just like a mortal girl.

'I do not want to lose you, love,' she whispered. 'Take no risks while hunting. Wolves, lions, bears are too fierce. Hunt only small creatures my darling, leave dangerous beasts alone.' And she pressed herself against him, all her goddess power gone.

Alone in the forest one day, Adonis came upon a wild boar. He smiled and lifted his spear, 'What a marvellous creature! And safe to hunt. Venus said nothing of boar.' Adonis gave chase, hurling his spear. But the spear fell short, piercing the boar on its flank. The boar bellowed, turned and charged, savagely burying its tusks into Adonis's thigh. Adonis cried out and fell to the ground. Venus flew to his side and found red blood spreading out around her beloved. She tore off her robe, pressed it to the gaping wound and tried to stem the flow. She took Adonis in her lap and held him tight, but his blood pumped away, draining into the earth. His face became pale and then his breathing stopped. Adonis died in Venus's arms.

'Curse you cruel fate for taking my loved one!' cried Venus. 'My grief shall never end, it will be remembered forever.'

Adonis's blood began to bubble, to bloom and to change into a deep, red flower. The anemone. Fragile crimson petals hung loosely from a stem. The anemone would be her memorial.

The anemone is the wind-flower and does not live long. As soon as the flower blooms and opens, the merest gust of breeze catches the petals and, shaken by the wind, the anemone is blown away. But each spring the blood-red anemone returns, and every time it blooms and fades, Venus loves and loves and loves, and never stops loving Adonis.

Pachamama

Inca, Andes

Bend down and take a pinch of soil between finger and thumb, look at it closely, feel its texture, breathe in its smell, taste it. This is her, Pachamama, from whom all life springs. Catch a snowflake on your tongue. Pick up a rock and rub the surface to reveal its buried traces. Look around you, Pachamama is everywhere.

She is Mother Earth, all is born from her, all returns to her. The wind is her breath, trees and grass her hair, the soil is her flesh, rocks her bones, flowing water is her blood. Pachamama is with us in every moment. She is the World Mother who creates life, spread out beneath us, rising above us. We live upon her and depend on her.

Find a hollow in a rock, fill it with flowers, water, flame and honour her. Spill beer on the ground in libation so that all may be fertile. Offer herbs so that she will give you a long life. Thank her as you take food from her body. Ask for her blessing and protection for your fields and families, your herds and home. But if you take too much, beware. If you remove the precious metals from her body then Pachamama will warn you with rumbles and reverberations, with fractures in land and fissures in cities, with floods and forest fires. Do not forget the one who gives life, all gifts come from her generous body. Kneel down, kiss the earth and remember Pachamama.

Quechua people honour Pachamama in festivals and celebrations throughout the year.

Cybele, Magna Mater

Roman

How many mothers are there? Millions, as many as there are children. But there is only one Cybele, the Magna Mater, who is childless. Or did the Great Mother father a child? Was Cybele a black meteorite that fell to earth? Did Cybele emerge from an underground cavern deep beneath a mountain? Or was Cybele the wild child of Sky and Earth?

Cybele was born both male and female, hermaphrodite. Cybele had breasts, cock, clit and androgynous power. Cybele loved to run, bounding over rocks with goats, sprinting over meadows with ponies, racing in a chariot pulled by lions. And Cybele loved to dance, whirling into a frenzy that drew gods, humans, nature into the dance, whipping everything into a trance. Gods and goddesses were afraid of Cybele's power, it was disturbing and it disturbed creation. They all agreed, Cybele had to be stopped. Bacchus brought a flask of his strongest wine and urged Cybele to drink, until Cybele slumped to the ground asleep. Then gods and goddesses sliced off Cybele's penis and tossed it into a muddy swamp. Gods and goddesses washed their hands and wrapped Cybele in a flowing robe. Cybele's uncontrollable power had been castrated.

Or had it? As soon as Cybele had recovered from the hangover, Cybele ran off into the woods, howling with wolves, growling with lions. Cybele's robes ripped at the thigh, Cybele could run faster! Panthers let Cybele sleep in their dens, leopards brought Cybele food. Wherever Cybele went nature flourished, grass grew, flowers bloomed, wild creatures came close, animals gave birth. Cybele became Guardian of the Forest, Mother of the Wilderness, Goddess of Nature, Mother Earth.

As for the phallus, it sank down to the bottom of the swamp and was buried in thick mud. Roots wriggled out of the penis and reached down into the dark water, shoots burst from it and shot towards the light. An almond tree grew from the severed organ. The tree was fragrant and strong. One day, a river nymph found her way into the swamp, came upon the almond tree and breathed in its scent. The nymph climbed out of the muddy water and plucked almond blossoms. She sat beneath the tree with the flowers in her lap. She wove the blossoms into a crown and placed it on her head. She felt warmth spread over her head and her cheeks flushed. She wove flowers into a necklace and hung the garland around her neck. Warmth spread to her chest, belly, back. The river nymph conceived from the potent blossoms of the almond tree. And a child grew inside her. Nine months later, she gave birth to a baby boy. He was as sweet as a nut and fragrant as a flower. The nymph named the boy Attis. Then gave the child to some shepherds to raise and swam away.

Years passed. And one day Cybele was running through the meadows and came upon a shepherd lad. He was tending his flock and playing a reed pipe. Cybele recognised something and sat down beside him.

'I know you. You are part of me.' Cybele took his hand, ran it over breast, belly, thigh. 'You came from me. You belong to me. You are mine and will always be mine.'
Cybele hugged him tight, then lifted him to his feet and began to dance. Cybele whirled Attis into a trance.

Attis, overwhelmed, swore, 'I am yours. I will be loyal to you for eternity.' After that Attis followed Cybele everywhere.

Until Attis met a human girl, a princess, and truly fell in love. This human love was so sweet, like a cloud of blossom love filled Attis, and he forgot Cybele and his promise. It was as though Cybele had never existed. The couple married in haste. But at the wedding feast, the ground trembled, tables and chairs shook, the sky went dark. The guests thought it was an earthquake and were about to run to the open fields for safety, when Cybele appeared, eyes bulging, mouth open, hair matted, clothes torn. Cybele let out a terrible howl and the sound filled everyone. All the guests were infected with crazed jealousy. They started picking up food and furniture and throwing it at the bride and groom. Cybele turned everyone mad, driving the guests into a frenzy. They destroyed the banquet, then fell upon the innocent princess and tore her to pieces. The wedding guests murdered the bride.

Attis ran into the hills screaming. He threw himself down beneath a pine tree. And thrashing about in a fit of insanity, took up a sharp stone and smashed at his groin. He hacked at his cock, cutting it away. Attis castrated himself. He rid himself of the part of his body that had betrayed him, the part that had been un-loyal. His blood flowed across the dusty ground, soaking into the roots of the pine tree. By the time Cybele arrived, Attis was dead, his body slumped at the foot of the tree. Cybele wept and clung to his bloodied body. Two lions came to comfort the goddess and sat down either side of Cybele.

'This pine tree will be forever sacred to you,' Cybele said. 'Nourished by your blood, it will honour you on hillsides and in wild places. Shepherds pipes will summon your spirit, my dances and songs will raise you up again. You are mine and will always be mine.'

Cybele's ceremonies spread. The goddess's priests, the Galli, carried pine branches in procession. They played reed pipes, the shrill sound leading them into ecstatic dancing. They beat themselves and each other with pine branches until they bled. They entered a trance and at the height of their ecstasy they castrated themselves, offering their sex to the goddess, their blood flowing like rain, making everything grow. The Galli had become both Cybele and Attis. Castration gave them Cybele's androgynous power. They grew their hair, wore flowing robes, hung amulets around their necks and wrists, made crowns of pine cones and blossom. Cybele's priests had become one with the goddess.

Cybele's cult grew, until the leaders of Rome were threatened. But Cybele's followers would not be stopped. Cybele became Magna Mater, the Great Mother, who protected girls, eased the pain of childbirth, healed the sick and shielded soldiers. Cybele's rituals became so popular they were eventually approved by the Roman state. Cybele was worshipped in temples and caves with altars of black stone and statues of Cybele wearing a stone menhir, a mountain, as a headdress. Cybele's temples were the place where all participants could be reborn. Magna Mater, roaring, wild, childless, father! Cybele was everything a mother should not, but could be.

The cult of Cybele originated in Anatolia and spread through Greece and Rome. This story is also a variant of Venus and Adonis. And is related to the myths of Ishtar and Isis.

Oshun, Sweet Water

Yoruba, Nigeria

Listen to her melodies rippling and splashing, the river is the Goddess Oshun playing. Watch her dancing, singing, bathe in her sweet water, be healed. But do not forget her.

The River Osun flows from the hilly forests above Osogbo down to the Lagos Lagoon and out to the sea. Along the banks of the river are sacred groves and shrines where you may meet the ancestors, commune with the spirits, get lost, be found, participate in old rituals and enter deep tranquillity. Goddess Oshun is the Mother of Fertility and without her nothing flows.

After the world had been created Oshun got left behind. Dust storms, hurricanes and fires swept across Earth destroying everything. Supreme Being Olodumare gathered the gods and said, 'Someone is missing. Where is our Goddess? Where is Oshun?' The gods looked about and the one female deity was not among them.

'Creation will not work without her. There will be no balance. Nothing will grow!' cried Olodumare. 'We need Oshun. She must not be forgotten. Find her at once!'

The gods found Oshun standing alone in the centre of a whirlwind, flames and dust raging around her. Her eyes were closed, her arms outstretched, her hands open and she was murmuring. She was summoning her vital power. The gods watched as droplets formed on her fingertips, liquid trickled down her hands. She chanted and water gushed from her palms. She swayed and a stream ran down her arms. Her voice soared and a river flowed from between her legs. Oshun brought forth water, sweet water. Her sweet water washed away the dust, put out the fires, calmed the wind. Her waters flowed and the ground turned green, plants sprang up, life emerged. The gods bowed and begged for forgiveness. It was Oshun alone, Mother of Fertility, who brought life to Earth. Nothing would exist without her sweet water.

Oshun's waters wound through hills and forests, filling lakes, running all the way to the sea. The goddess walked along a river. She came to a glade where the river became shallower and wider, tumbling over rocks, gathering in deep pools. The river was fringed by trees dipping great roots into the water.

The Mother of Fertility said, 'This is the place where you will remember me. Build a city here and honour me here. My sweet waters will heal and protect you. But if you want life and fertility, do not forget me.'

The city of Osogbo was built on the banks of the River Osun. In the heart of the city is a sacred grove dedicated to the Goddess Oshun. It is a place of mystery, with spirits carved into rocks and trees, where offerings are made to the Goddess Oshun. The goddess is evoked in songs, prayers and rituals. And in return, Oshun bestows health, fertility, flow. Her waters transform the world. But if her prayers are not remembered, if the Goddess Oshun is forgotten, then her waters are not so sweet. She might withhold her water so that the ground becomes parched and cracked, rivers dry up and nothing grows. Or she might make it rain without stopping, so rivers burst their banks and floods destroy crops and homes.

'Keep the balance, maintain the flow,' she cries. 'Never forget me.'

Oshun is a living goddess and her shrines and rituals are an important part of Yoruba culture. There are other Yoruba myths about Oshun where she is jealous and vengeful, showing the tempestuous and dangerous aspects of water.

Green Tara

Princess Yeshe Dawe lived millions of years in the past, in another world system, long before the cycle of human existence that we are part of had begun. Yeshe Dawe was extremely rich and beautiful, but she did not care about her looks or possessions. Like the meaning of her name, 'moon of primordial awareness', she was only interested in deepening her awareness. Her one wish was to attain enlightenment and so she spent her time in prayer.

When Yeshe woke, she opened her chamber windows that looked out onto the kingdom and snowy mountains beyond and placed a cushion on the window sill. She sat with one foot curled beneath her, the other foot outstretched, her right hand open pointing to the earth, her left hand raised and pointing to the sky with her thumb and ring finger touching. Then Yeshe would close her eyes and sink into stillness. She thought that if she could sit in silent contemplation and be very still, she might have a chance of liberating the suffering of other souls. She would meditate before breakfast, before lunch, before supper and again before sleep.

All around her the palace would go about its business. Her mother, the Queen, would be dressed in silks and jewels. Her father, the king, would hold meetings, greet guests, make decisions. Food would be prepared, banquets held, music played, gifts given. But Yeshe barely took part in it. She would excuse herself as soon as she could, return to her cushion and close her eyes.

Early one morning she was sitting in her window, when two young monks passed by. They stopped and stared at the princess. They sniggered, then began to laugh until they were bent double with laughter. Yeshe slowly opened her eyes and looked at them.

'Why are you laughing?' she asked.

'Pray for yourself!' chuckled the monks. 'Before you pray for others!' And they laughed even louder.

'Why?' said the princess.

'Pray that you're born again as a man! Because you will never attain enlightenment as a woman.'

Yeshe began to giggle, then joined the monks bent double with howls of laughter. The monks looked nervously at the princess.

'Why are you laughing?' they asked.

Yeshe stopped laughing and said, 'Only weak-minded worldlings would see gender as barrier to enlightenment.'

The monks fell silent and Yeshe continued, 'Enlightenment is for all, it makes no difference who you are. But thank you for your advice. I will pray. I will pray that I am always a woman. That I return as a woman again and again until the wheel of suffering has ended.' And Princess Yeshe Dawe closed her eyes and sank back into meditation.

Yeshe meditated without stopping and let nothing disturb her. Yeshe's prayers liberated a hundred souls before breakfast, several hundred before lunch, even more before supper and still more before sleep. Yeshe mediated without stopping for hundreds, thousands, millions, for ten million years. She came back again and again as a woman and her prayers relieved ten million beings from suffering.

Until the Buddha of the time, Tonyo Drupa, who was a quite different Buddha from the Buddha of our time, appeared before her. 'Your destiny is to be born again in another world system yet to come, far into the future. You will become the Goddess Tara. The word tar means to cross. And the Goddess Tara will help souls cross the ocean of existence, like a star you will guide souls from birth to death.'

Billions of years later, when our world cycle had begun, a young man, Chenrezig, was walking through a city. All around him he saw people who were hungry, homeless, ill. There was so much division and hatred, human beings no longer helped each other or worked together, the world was fuelled by sheer greed. Chenrezig walked out of the city, climbed to the summit of a hill, sat down and closed his eyes. He began praying ceaselessly, repeating mantras to liberate souls from suffering, meditating without stopping to set all beings free. Centuries later, Chenrezig opened his eyes and in the distance he saw fires blazing, war raging. All around him there was death, famine, storms, drought and fear. Centuries of prayer had not been enough to stop the suffering. Chenrezig began to weep. Tears ran down his cheeks and fell onto the ground. Chenrezig's tears flowed down into the valley below. The tears covered the ground, filled the valley and turned into a lake. A lake of tears.

Then one day a lotus leaf appeared, floating on the surface of the lake. In the centre of the leaf was the white bud of a lotus flower. The flower slowly opened and sweet perfume filled the air. Chenrezig wiped the tears from his cheeks and watched. Sitting in the centre of the flower was a woman with green skin.

'I am Tara. I have come to help you accomplish your mission more swiftly. We will work together to stop the suffering of the world.'

Tara sat in the lotus flower with one foot curled beneath her. Her other foot was outstretched so she was ready to step into the realms of suffering at any moment, unafraid to step into the world of pain. Her right hand was open and pointing down, offering support to all. Her left hand was raised, pointing the way to wisdom, her thumb and ring finger touching to reveal the jewel of understanding. Tara closed her eyes and joined Chenrezig in mediation. Together their prayers freed and guided souls from birth to death, steering souls across the ocean of existence.

As Goddess Tara meditated, her mind became a mirror that reflected the whole world. Her eternal being refracted light, unfolding a rainbow of colours that constantly shifted across space. Until the Goddess Tara appeared simultaneously in different colours and forms, ready to help all. White Tara heals, dispels upset, bestows grace. Red Tara is there for all who long for love, turning raw passion into compassion. Yellow Tara brings wealth and prosperity. Black Tara gives power. Blue Tara embodies ferocious energy, destroying obstacles and transmuting anger. All the colours fuse together and make Green Tara. Green Tara brings protection and release from fear. Green Tara is the Universal Mother of the World, helping us cross the ocean of existence, soothing sorrow, showing the way, regenerating the world through wisdom.

Tara is a major goddess in both Hindu and Buddhist tradition, particularly in Tibet. There are numerous tales linked to her origin where she appears in both peaceful and wrathful forms. These myths are found in India, South East Asia, China and Tibet. There are special Tara practices, reciting her mantras and visualising her forms, which allow you to see your true essence and be filled with her light.

Demeter and Persephone

Greece

The procession followed the Sacred Way out of Athens, through the hills, over narrow stone bridges, along dusty tracks to Eleusis. The crowds were singing, praying, carrying flowers. They were following a mother searching for her lost daughter, they were going to participate in the Mysteries. And like mother and daughter, they would go down into the unknown in order to return. Initiates would make sacrifices of wild pigs, undertake purification rituals, fast, dress in unworn robes, dance around the Maiden's Well and drink holy barley water. Only then could they enter the darkness of the secret chamber and take part in the most sacred rite of all. There, initiates would witness what must never be revealed, never ever spoken of. They are blessed who have seen such things.

Demeter is the Goddess of Grain, Mother of the Harvest, the very matter of the earth. She has one daughter, her beloved Persephone. Who was the maiden's father? It might have been Demeter's own brothers, Zeus or Poseidon. Perhaps it was Dionysus. Or the hunter Iasion. All took Demeter against her will. Iasion raped the goddess in the furrows of a thrice-ploughed field. When Poseidon pursued her, Demeter changed herself into a mare and hid among a herd of horses. But Poseidon changed into a stallion, circled the mare and mounted her. Fury filled Demeter and she transformed into

Erinyes, Goddess of Anger. Righteous rage seized the entire world. And the fury only ceased when Demeter washed it away in the River Ladon. From one or all of these rapes, Demeter bore her daughter.

One day, Persephone was walking through the meadows with her friends Athene and Artemis. The maidens were picking spring flowers, filling their arms with crocus, violets, iris, hyacinths. Persephone picked and picked, breathing in the heavenly scent. She gathered flowers into the folds of her gown and left her friends far behind. Then she saw a strange flower with a hundred petals. She bent to pick it but its roots dug deep into the earth. Persephone pulled at the stem and the ground shook, the earth opened up and a gaping hole appeared. A few wild pigs grazing nearby tumbled down the hole, disappearing into the darkness.

There was a rumble and four black horses charged out of the depths dragging a golden chariot. Holding the reins was Hades, Lord of the Dead. He pulled the horses to a stop, 'What beauty is this? A living girl to be my bride! I am so lonely in the underworld. You will light up my kingdom.' Hades reached out, plucked Persephone from the ground and pulled her into his chariot. Persephone cried for help but her voice was lost on the wind. The Goddess Hekate, sitting in her cave wearing her silver headdress, heard the maiden's cry. She looked up from her work for a moment, but saw nothing. Hades cracked his whip and the horses hurtled down to the realm of stone.

The horses raced beneath towering rocks, beside boiling lakes and smouldering fields of lava. Then the horses rose into the air and flew above a cold, green river, the River Styx that divides the world of the living from the world of the dead. On the other side of the river were the iron gates of the underworld, protected by the three-headed monster Kerberus, guardian of hell. The beast saw its master and sank to the ground, bowing its three heads, and the gates swung open. Hades led Persephone into his underworld palace. The stone walls were shot through with glistening seams of silver and gold. The Lord of the Dead took Persephone to a throne studded with jewels.

'Now you are Queen of the Underworld,' he said. 'All this belongs to you.'

Persephone did not speak, she refused to eat, drink or sleep and would only weep.

The wind carried the faint sound of Persephone's cry to the Goddess Demeter. She felt a sharp pain in her heart and knew it was her daughter. Demeter wrapped herself in a cloak and took a burning torch in each hand. The goddess walked through long, hot days wandering the earth, searching for her daughter. At night the goddess held her torches high, but did not find her dear Persephone. Demeter came to a crossroads and standing in the centre was a woman wearing a shimmering headdress and holding a torch. She was turning, shining her light down each road, illuminating the way ahead. It was Hekate, Goddess of the Three Ways.

'Lady Demeter, Bringer of Ripeness, Giver of Gifts, I know what you are searching for and you will not find it on these roads. I heard a maiden cry, but I did not see who took your daughter. Let us speak to Helios, the Sun God sees everything.'

The two goddesses stood before the Sun God. Helios nodded, 'Hades took her in broad daylight.'

Demeter sobbed.

'Why weep?' said Helios. 'This is a good marriage, Persephone will be Queen.'

Demeter let out a howl.

'This is not good or a marriage. She has been abducted, stolen. Both mother and daughter raped, taken against our will. This crime will be paid for.'

Demeter's weeping turned to rage. She wandered the earth howling, her hair turned grey with grief and her divine glory disappeared. Until no one recognised her. The great goddess had become an ordinary old woman. She came to the Kingdom of Eleusis and, worn out, sat down beside the Maiden's Well. Four girls carrying brass pitchers came to draw water. They were the King's daughters, Kallidike, Kleisidike, Demo and Kallithoe. They did not recognise the goddess and asked, 'Where have you come from, Lady? We have not seen you before?'

'Dear children,' said Demeter, 'I was taken by pirates, they travelled here and I escaped.'

Demeter began to cry.

'Come and rest in the shade of our palace,' said the girls.

Demeter was taken to the palace kitchen, but could not stop weeping. Kitchen maid Iambe offered her warm bread and barley water with mint. Demeter refused and sat with her head in her hands. The kitchen maid did not insist, instead Iambe told a joke. Demeter lifted her head. Iambe told a ruder joke with sound effects. Demeter stopped weeping. Then Iambe raised her blouse and shook her hips. A smile flickered across Demeter's lips. Iambe lowered her skirt, opened her legs and revealed her womb. Demeter saw a baby gurgling, pink and cosy inside Iambe's womb! Demeter laughed too. Then accepted the cool drink.

'Wise Iambe, your golden tongue will be remembered thousands of years from now.'

Iambe laughed even harder, why would a simple kitchen maid ever be remembered!

Demeter felt refreshed. In return for royal hospitality, she taught the princesses the skills of needlework, of making patterns with thread. She took care of the princesses' mother, Queen Metanira, who had just given birth to a baby boy. The goddess took the baby in her lap, breathed sweet breath on him and fed him from her own breast. At night, when the Queen was asleep, Demeter would light a fire from her torch and place the baby like a log into the flames. Queen Metanira admired how her boy grew so fast and seemed to glow with health. One night the Queen woke to the smell of smoke, she peeped from her chamber and saw Demeter placing the baby in a fire. The Queen screamed with terror and the flames went out. The Queen rushed to save her son and found her baby was completely unharmed.

Demeter began to change, her grey hair turned gold, her aged body regained its goddess glory, filling the room with divine light.

'I was not harming your child,' said the goddess, 'I was giving your son immortality. Now he will die like any mortal. But because he lay in my lap, his life will be blessed.'

'Great Goddess of Grain, forgive me, I did not know it was you,' said Queen Metanira. 'What may we do for you?'

'Build me a temple above the Maiden's Well. Create a dancing floor on the spur of the hill. Follow my sacred rites, honour my mysteries. This will comfort my soul.'

Demeter continued searching and asking. She walked across earth for a whole year and did not find her daughter. High up in the meadows she met a young lad, Triptolemus, tending his animals. He showed Demeter a deep hole.

'I lost my pigs down there.'

Demeter stared into the darkness. This was where her daughter had gone. She placed a stalk of barley in the lad's hand, 'Plant this, you will become rich.'

Triptolemus had no idea how a single plant could make him rich. But he went home, dug the soil and planted the stalk.

Demeter fell to her knees and cried, 'Curse you, cruel Earth! You do not deserve to bear fruit if you keep my daughter underground.' A cold wind began to blow. The wind tore leaves from trees and plants from roots. Bitter cold spread across the world and nothing grew. Flowers, fruits and barley lay hidden underground. The great goddess wrapped herself in her cloak and sat weeping, waiting for the world to die of hunger. It was a year of biting misery, winter without end.

The gods begged Demeter to remove her curse.

'Bring my daughter,' she replied.

Zeus called his messenger, 'Hermes, my Swift One, find Persephone and bring her back so Demeter will make Earth green again.'

Hermes, with golden staff and winged sandals, flashed down to the realm of the dead and into Hades's shady kingdom.

Persephone was sitting on the jewelled throne with Hades beside her. She was no longer weeping and her radiant beauty filled the underworld with light. Hermes bowed, 'I come with a message. Zeus calls Persephone home. Earth is dying. Nothing grows. Hades, you must let her go.'

Hades was silent. Persephone held her breath, waiting for him to speak and the underworld waited too. At last Hades said, 'Persephone, flower of my life, I was so lonely before you came. I do not want to lose you. Even the rocks and stones love you. But father Zeus cannot be disobeyed.'

Persephone leapt to her feet. Then Hades clapped his hands, and a golden platter appeared heaped with pomegranate seeds.

'Wait, my Queen,' said Hades. 'All this time no food has passed your lips.' Hades held out the plate, 'Eat before you go. It will give you energy for your journey.'

The pomegranate seeds looked so red and plump they seemed to glow. Suddenly Persephone felt hungry. She reached out, took a seed and popped it into her mouth. She crushed the seed against her tongue and tangy juice burst inside her mouth. Persephone pressed two more seeds between her lips, then Hermes took her hand and they flew from dark to light.

Demeter looked up and there was her daughter! She flung her arms around Persephone and hugged her tight. Mother and daughter were reunited, they clasped hands and walked home. With each step Persephone took, green shoots of barley pushed out of the earth. Wheat grew thick around their ankles, corn rippled gold, tickling their legs. The air was filled with the sound of birds singing. Persephone had returned and spring had come at last.

Demeter spread the table with fresh bread, white cheese, dark olives and cool barley water. Hekate came to welcome Persephone home.

'I'm starving!' said Persephone, and she reached towards the food.

'You didn't eat, my daughter, did you?' asked Demeter. 'You didn't eat the food of the underworld?'

'No, Mother. No food passed my lips,' said Persephone, sucking on an olive stone. 'Except …'

'Except what?' said Demeter.

'Just three pomegranate seeds. Three tiny little seeds.'

Demeter began to cry.

'Oh, Persephone! The food of the dead must not pass the lips of the living. The living must not eat the food of the dead. For those three seeds I will lose you.'

For three months of each year Persephone returns to the underworld. Hades rejoices, he is no longer lonely, and the rocks and stones welcome back their queen. Persephone felt she had come home. But while Persephone is underground, winter comes to earth. It is cold and crops lie buried in the ground. Persephone spends three winter months in the underworld. Then ice melts, the ground grows soft and Persephone returns. Demeter hugs her daughter and spreads a feast of flowers. Earth bears fruit and we have spring again. Then Demeter picks the barley to make bread, knowing, like all mothers, that for anything to grow it must winter underground, knowing that life depends on death, laughter on tears, spring on winter.

As for Iambe's golden tongue, her jokes, poems, stories spread around the world and the iambic metre of poetry is still famous thousands of years later. And where Triptolemus planted the single stalk, a whole field of barley grew and he became rich.

All become mothers and all become daughters in the Eleusinian Mysteries. Initiates dance around the Maiden's Well in an endless circle, forever changing, old to young, young to old, mother to daughter, daughter to mother, the cycle repeated for eternity. And it is said that the most sacred rite of all, the secret never to be spoken of, was when a basket was opened and a single stalk of barley was held up in the lamplight. Then, the minds and hearts of the initiates would burst open, become illuminated, and they would truly comprehend how all life depends on Persephone's journey.

Even though the myth of Persephone is not part of religious life in contemporary Greece, the story is still remembered. On New Year's Eve people crack pomegranates on their doorsteps to bring good luck for the coming year. At weddings pomegranates are broken and the seeds rolled across the ground to bring happiness and fertility. At funerals a dish made of pomegranate seeds is prepared in honour of the dead. In some villages in Sicily, villagers cut down spring branches and shape them into figures of Persephone, then they parade around the fields with her figure to encourage growth. And you eat Demeter each morning when you eat cereal! The English word for cereal comes from the Roman version of Demeter, the Goddess Ceres. In Greece, the word for cereal is Dimitra!

Queen Mother
of the West

China

High up between heaven and earth, in the misty regions of the Kunlun Mountains, is the Western Paradise. This is where Xi Wang Mu resides. The Queen Mother of the West wears a headdress of tinkling jade, a rainbow dress with feathered sleeves and black dancing shoes decorated with phoenixes. Beneath her headdress her hair is matted and tangled, under her robe she has a leopard tail and inside her shoes are tiger claws. Xi Wang Mu can be peaceful and generous or she can growl and snarl. She is the mother who gives and takes. Goddess of Epidemics, bringing illness and disease. Goddess of Immortality, giving health and eternal life. Her palace is made of pure gold decorated with gem stones. Beside it is an orchard with a single peach tree, its trunk is three thousand miles wide. The tree bears peaches that take three thousand years to grow and another three thousand years to ripen. These precious peaches contain the elixir of immortality.

Xi Wang Mu was the bearer of a great secret, she obtained immortality by feeding the yin within herself. To do this she had lovers, many lovers! She seduced young men and boys and as they gave themselves to her, at the moment of their greatest pleasure she took their energy, pulled the yin out of their bodies and absorbed it into her own. As the young men withdrew themselves from the body of the goddess, she glowed with beauty but they felt ill. Xi Wang Mu would pick up her lute, sing and play to them, recite poems. The young men would lie back to listen and be overcome by agonising pain. Xi Wang Mu would calmly drink a glass of milk as her lover died. Then she would bathe and prepare to take another lover. Xi Wang Mu stored the yin inside herself, building it up, amassing such power that she became eternally young, radiant, immortal.

The Queen Mother of the West accumulated so much yin, she was able to bestow the gift of eternal life on others. The ancient documents that tell this story were written by men, and they ask that the reader keeps Xi Wang Mu's great secret. They beg the reader not to spread the story of how she gained immortal life, in case other women get inspired and decide to copy the goddess!

Once every six thousand years the peaches ripen and the Queen Mother holds her birthday party. She flies around the world on the back of a white crane or a phoenix, or rides on the back of a tiger to give out the invitations to her Feast of Peaches. She sends her flock of bluebirds to deliver the message that it is her birthday at last. Emperors, queens, generals, tricksters, thieves all want to attend. Most fail to arrive, even more fail to undertake the strict conditions that are demanded before partaking of the peaches. For the lucky ones who make their way into the Queen Mother's palace, they bow before Xi Wang Mu. She is seated with her cosmic attendants, the three-legged crow who lives on the sun, the hare with pestle and mortar who lives on the moon, pounding the nectar of immortality. These creatures give the Queen Mother power over the sun and moon. The guests take their places and the Queen Mother's companions, the Jade Maidens, serve them a feast of bear paws, monkey lips, dragon liver and phoenix marrow. Then the maidens play music on jade sounding stones, phoenix chimes, thunder flutes and cloud harmony mouth organs. The sounds echo into far distant space and the maidens whirl, turning their fans, their long sleeves fluttering. Xi Wang Mu joins the dance, opening the feathered sleeves of her robe like wings. Then the Jade Maidens lift the baskets of peaches for all the guests to see and a sweet summer perfume fills the air. The peaches are served. And as soon as their ripe flesh touches human lips, guests lose all sense of time. A guest lifts a hand or turns their head and years pass. A thousand years are gone in the flicker of an eye. Millions of years vanish as a cricket chirps.

When the guests finally leave their horses have turned to white bone, their carriages have rotted and collapsed. Some never leave, they climb the peach tree following spirits and deities up the sky-ladder of the massive tree trunk into the upper realms. But the Queen Mother takes up a watering can and a bucket of fresh compost and goes to tend her peach tree for the next six thousand years.

Xi Wang Mu is the most important goddess in Daoism. There are many stories of emperors who tried to get the immortal peaches from Xi Wang Mu, some of whom she had passionate affairs with. When women reach fifty, they honour the Queen Mother of the West to gain her blessing. Her image often appears on the backs of mirrors, so that the one who looks will be eternally beautiful.

The Seven Scorpions of Isis

Egypt

The Mistress of Magic and Speaker of Spells gave birth to her longed for baby boy. She named him Horus, Far-Above-One, the soaring Hawk God. As Ra had commanded, Isis pressed Horus to her chest, placed her heart over his heart and passed Ra's secret name to her son. Then she walked with her baby into the papyrus marshes. She would bring her son up in secret, teaching him everything she knew until he was old enough to kill Set and avenge his father's murder.

Isis nursed the baby among the tall reeds. From time to time she would go to fetch food. Early one morning she wrapped Horus in a spell of protection, asked the marsh nymphs to watch over him and left him sleeping in the shade of the rushes. Then Isis set out with her army of seven scorpions. Three scorpions went ahead, Petet, Tjetet and Matet cleared the way, ensuring the path was safe and nothing would hinder the goddess. Two more, Mesetet and Mesetetef, walked either side of Isis to protect her. And the largest scorpions, Befen and Tefen, followed in her wake, protecting the goddess from behind.

'Caution, my army!' instructed Isis. 'Stay alert for Set. He could be hiding anywhere. Do not speak to anyone on the way.'

Isis and her seven scorpions made their way out of the marshes, along the river, under the hot sun to the town of Two Sandals on the Nile delta. They walked down a dusty road, past a huge mansion. A rich woman opened a grand door, saw the seven scorpions with their tails lifted and stings held high and cried, 'Get back! Stay away, you dangerous creatures!' She did not recognise the Goddess Isis and slammed the door in her face.

The seven scorpions were insulted and lifted their stings higher. Isis continued walking through the town and they passed a tumbledown hut. A poor girl peeped out of a broken door and saw the seven scorpions with their tails and stings. She did not recognise the goddess and said, 'I don't have much but please come in and rest here.'

Isis sat in the shade of the hut, drank water and shared the girl's bread. But the seven scorpions did not rest, they wanted revenge. The scorpions all placed their stings on top of Tefen's sting and deposited their venom, loading Tefen's sting with sevenfold poison. Tefen crawled out of the hut, down the road and under the rich woman's door. Tefen scuttled across the floor to a baby lying in a cradle. Tefen lifted his sting and speared the baby's chubby thigh. The baby howled, sevenfold poison burned through the child's skin, into his veins, all the way to his heart. The poison was so hot the cradle burst into flames! The noblewoman dragged her child from the burning cradle. The baby was bright red from head to foot and barely breathing. The woman ran into the street, screaming for help. But no one came. She pleaded and wailed but all doors remained shut and her cries were unanswered.

Isis heard the woman's sobs. 'I know what it means to be a mother,' she said and stepped out into the street. 'I will not let your child die!'

Isis began to change, a brilliant crown appeared on her head, a throne holding two curved horns of the moon supporting a shining disk of the sun.

'Come to the Mistress of Magic, she never slams the door. Come to the Speaker of Spells, she turns no one away. Come to the mother who knows the secret of restoring life!'

The woman bowed and placed the limp, burned body of her son in the goddess's hands. Isis put her palms on his chest, she breathed cool air onto his hot flesh, then she cried, 'Petet, Tjetet,

Matet, Mesetet, Mesetetef, Befen, Tefen let go, release. Seven scorpions stand back. My scorpions let your poison fall to the ground. Great poison come out. Sevenfold poison depart. Poison of Tefen be gone!' The baby breathed in and opened his eyes. The redness faded, the boy gurgled, his skin healed. The boy smiled and was well again. The woman hugged her son tight. 'Great Goddess I did not recognise you. I am so ashamed. Forgive me.'

The woman went home and gathered up all her precious necklaces and bracelets, her golden earrings, her jewelled anklets and engraved rings. And she offered the jewels to Isis. The goddess took them and turned to the poor girl, 'You don't have a child, and yet you know what it is to be a mother. You opened the door and helped. May all be a mother like you.' And Isis gave her the jewels. Then the seven scorpions surrounded the goddess and they marched back into the marshes.

Variants of this myth are found in cultures across the world. This is one of the very oldest versions ever written down.

Lakshmi, Mother of Prosperity

India

If you are starting a new job or moving house, taking exams or going on a journey, ask for Lakshmi's blessing. The Mother of Prosperity will watch over you and bring success. Call on Lakshmi if you have lost your keys or cannot find your purse, the Goddess of Good Fortune will help. When you are embarking on anything new, the loving mother Lakshmi will bring you luck.

Lakshmi was born at the beginning of time, when the gods and goddesses churned the ocean for the cream of life, amrita, the nectar of immortality. One sip of this ambrosia and the gods would never die. The gods churned the ocean with a mountain as their churning stick. The King of Snakes, Vasuki wrapped himself around the mountain as their churning rope. The gods could not churn the ocean alone and offered the demons a sip of immortality if they would help. The gods held the snake's head and the demons held its tail, together they pulled the snake, the mountain twirled and the sea churned. The snake became so hot, flames flashed and boiling poison streamed from its jaws.

Shiva, the Destroyer, caught the poison in his mouth and held it there to protect the world. His throat turned blue and he has been holding the poison in his throat ever since. The mountain spun so fast it bore a hole through the centre of the earth. Vishnu, the Preserver, turned himself into a turtle and plunged to the bottom of the sea. He rested the peak of the mountain on the back of his unbreakable shell. The mountain whirled smoothly, the sea frothed, whipping up white crested waves. The ocean turned to creamy milk and treasures rose to the surface.

First, a slender silver moon appeared. Shiva fixed it in his black hair where it shines, making the oceans rise and fall. Next, the wish-fulfilling cow, Surabhi, appeared. She grants wishes from the everlasting milk that flows from her udders. Then a woman emerged from the creamy froth. She was sitting on a pink lotus flower, wearing a golden robe and shining crown. She had four arms, two hands raised to the sky holding scented flowers, and two hands pointing to the earth with gold coins pouring from

her fingertips. Two elephants rose up beside her, pouring streams of water over her dark hair. Lakshmi, Goddess of Good Fortune, Mother of Prosperity, had been born. Of course, all the gods wanted to marry her but Lakshmi refused.

'I will choose,' she said.

The milky ocean began to thicken and turned to cream. An old man carrying a golden goblet appeared. It was the wise physician holding amrita, the ambrosia of eternal life. But the demons rushed forward, grabbed the goblet and disappeared with it down to the underworld. Vishnu, the Preserver, disguised himself as a woman and seduced the demons, tricking them into giving up the goblet. At last, the gods and goddesses drank the nectar of immortality and received eternal life. They turned to Vishnu and said, 'Vishnu, Maintainer of Life, how can we thank you?'

Before Vishnu could speak, Lakshmi stepped forward, 'I have chosen. I will take the Preserver Vishnu as my husband. He is my equal.'

Vishnu could not resist and took the goddess in his arms. They lay down together on his couch, a thousand-headed serpent, which floats in the endless ocean. Lakshmi and Vishnu fell asleep, floating in space, dreaming the dream of the world. Vishnu wakes from time to time to help those in trouble. And Lakshmi wakes too and is always beside him. When Vishnu became Rama, Lakshmi was Sita. When Vishnu became Krishna, Lakshmi was Radha. The Mother of Prosperity is always there spreading hope, bringing abundance.

On the night of the Lakshmi puja welcome the Goddess of Good Fortune. This is the night that Lakshmi roams the earth. Clean your house, fill it with flowers, make honey cakes, pile plates with sweets and open all the windows and doors so the goddess can enter. Place little lights, diyas, on windowsills and door steps. The glowing flames are a path for the goddess to travel along. Sing Lakshmi's praises, tell her stories and invite the goddess in. If the Mother of Prosperity passes through your home she will bring you health and wealth and fill your home with good fortune. The next morning when you sweep the floor, you might find a few gold coins among the flower petals.

Lakshmi reminds us that wealth is all around us, the beauty of nature makes us rich. And tell the stories of Lakshmi, because for us poor humans there is no immortality, we were not able to sip the precious amrita. But it is said that those who have heard Lakshmi's stories will be revived and blessed for the rest of their lives.

Lakshmi has many stories about her various incarnations beside Vishnu. These are beyond the scope of this book. But you can find her stories as she incarnates as: Padma; Dharani; Sita; Radha and Rukmini. Lakshmi is also known as Sri, so you will find more about her under this name too.

Crone

Asase Yaa,
Old Woman Earth

Ashanti, Ghana

Old Woman Earth is ancient yet eternally young. Asase Yaa was there when time started and is the Mother of Life. All creation emerged from her womb. She gave birth to nature, gods, creatures, human beings. The Mother of Life loves all her children but she cannot help loving her son, the spider Anansi, the most. He makes her chuckle as he spins threads of deceit and trickery. And he makes her nod her head in agreement as he weaves wisdom into his web. The Mother of Life is always among us. Worship her in the fields as you dig the soil, plant seeds, tend your gardens, gather flowers, pick fruit, harvest vegetables.

Old Woman Earth makes everything grow. Thank her as you leave the soil to rest for winter. If you want to please Asase Yaa then stop working for one day each week, go outside and breathe her air, walk on her land. If you want the blessing of Asase Yaa then stop working on a Thursday. This is her sacred day and the goddess is named Yaa for it.

Old Woman Earth is ancient yet never dies. Asase Yaa is there when every life ends and is the Mother of Death. She takes us all back into her womb, returning us to our source deep underground. Old Woman Earth protects all who are buried within her, caring for each soul as if it were a newborn baby. She cradles us, rocks us and weighs up our lives. The Mother of Death is always among us. Worship her as you close your eyes and fall asleep, thank her when you wake to a new day. Old Woman Earth is the final judge and it is she who decides where our souls will go next. But do not despair, Asase Yaa is not a cruel mother. Around her neck is a green snake, coiled like an emerald jewel. Old Woman Earth knows the snake's secret, how to shed her skin and become young again. Mother of Death becomes Mother of Life without end and she bids us all to follow her. Sprinkle soil onto a seed and Old Woman Earth will be with you.

Asase Yaa is an important goddess in cultures across West and Central Africa, Guyana and the Caribbean, appearing in many mythologies, especially in the Akhan religions. She appears with Anansi in some folktales, sometimes he steals from her or tries to trick her but he never succeeds.

Baba Marta

Bulgaria

Baba Marta is coming! Grandma March is coming with a stick and a bent back. If you listen, you can hear her stick tap tapping. Baba Marta can be a sweet old lady who brings warm sunshine and spring flowers. Or she can be a grumpy old woman who brings icy winds and snow.

Baba Marta is the sister of Big Sechko, January, and Little Sechko, February. Baba Marta is always annoyed by her brothers, they leave such a mess! They ruin her washing, bring mud into the house, use up all the firewood, finish the pots of berry jam she had been storing since last summer and they cannot resist drinking her wine. The brothers change Baba Marta's mood in an instant: winds blow, grey clouds gather, rain comes and as they say in Bulgaria, 'Baba Marta lets winter back in!'

So get ready for the first of March. Baba Marta is coming and we want the spring! Clean your house, place a fresh embroidered cloth on the table and spread a feast. Everyone must make martenitsas, little red and white tassels. Red for the sun, white for the melting snow. Red for fertility, white for purity. Weave the threads together so they look like tiny figures, give them round heads and wide skirts. Tie the martenitsas to your clothes or hang them from a tree, the tassels will make her happy. She will tap her stick, join the party and bring the spring!

Wear your martenitsas until blossoms appear, until the stork returns, then you will know that Baba Marta has brought the spring and it is here to stay. Grandma March will not take it away again. Chestita Baba Marta – Happy Baba Marta!

Baba Marta is a living goddess and versions of her rituals and songs are celebrated beyond Bulgaria in the Balkans and surrounding countries.

Great Lady of the Night

Māori, New Zealand

When the sun sets you can see Hine-nui-te-pō glinting in the distance, in the place where sky and earth meet. That golden glint on the horizon are her eyes flashing, that orange glow her vulva shining, that red haze her womb opening and closing. The Great Lady of the Night is calling human beings back, back to their place of origin.

The Ancestress of All longed for humans to return, to travel the path of the setting sun and follow her down into the realms of her dark palace. But no one wanted to go, no one wanted to die and no one followed her. Death did not exist, everyone lived forever and they wanted to continue doing so. The Great Lady of the Night had been waiting since dawn, the dawn of time, for humans to return to her. And she was not in a hurry. She was already ancient and could wait forever. Hine-nui-te-pō lay dozing at the skyline, sure that death would come.

Humans watched from a distance and kept out of her way. Until Maui decided to visit his ancestress.

'I will conquer death!' he declared.

Maui, trickster, creator, had already made the sun slow down, fished up the islands of New Zealand with his enchanted hook and given fire to the people.

'I will journey into the very body of the Goddess of Death and return. I will enter her womb and come out of her mouth. I will reverse death so that no one will ever have to follow the Great Lady of the Night down into the dark!'

Maui threw off his clothes, revealing burnished tattoos that covered his body. He tied his magic weapon, the sacred jaw bone, around his waist. Then he set off to the place where sky meets earth. A few birds followed him, a fantail, a robin, a grey warbler. They flew around Maui, flitting back and forth, wondering what he was going to do. Maui walked into the golden light and approached the goddess. Hine-nui-te-pō was lying on her back with her legs wide open. Her hair, long strands of dark green kelp, was spread across her body. Her silver mouth, as pointed as a fish, hid the teeth of a barracuda. The Great Lady of the Night was asleep and snoring.

'This is going to be easy!' said Maui.

The birds fluttered about as Maui peered between Hine's legs. He saw a dark opening. A deep pit without end. A black hole. It was like looking into a grave, if only Maui had known what one looked like! Inside the hole Maui could just make out the shadowy shapes of something spikey. The Great Lady's vagina was filled with teeth! Ragged teeth made of sharp obsidian, jagged teeth made of pointed greenstone razors.

'Not so easy,' said Maui.

'Don't go in there,' chattered the birds. 'You'll be killed!'

'Shhh! My friends,' whispered Maui. 'Be quiet. Do not make a noise. We must not wake the Goddess of Death. When I have passed through her body and I am coming out of her mouth, then you can celebrate. When I have reversed death, then you can sing. When human beings live forever you can chirp and tweet as much as you like.'

Maui took the form of a rat.

'Too big,' chirruped the birds.

Maui took the form of a worm.

'Too tasty,' said the birds.

Maui took the form of a green caterpillar and the birds were silent.

Maui wriggled into Hine's dark vagina. Bolts of lightning flashed, illuminating towering teeth. The birds began to giggle. The caterpillar writhed between the jagged teeth. The birds clamped their beaks tight to stop themselves from laughing. The caterpillar squirmed deeper and deeper into the vagina between the razor-sharp greenstone fangs. The birds could not help themselves; they cackled loudly, they had never seen anything so funny and could not hold back any longer, they screeched, snorted and hopped about. The Great Lady of the Night was woken up by all the noise. She felt wriggling inside her. At last! She knew human beings would not be able to resist forever. The moment had finally come.

Hine-nui-te-pō closed her legs, slammed her thighs together tight and bit hard! She bit down. She crunched, she chewed, she gnawed, she chewed up Maui! And Maui met his death inside the great goddess's birth canal. Maui died in the place where he was born, the womb of the goddess. All human beings have followed Maui ever since, to the skyline in the distance into the sleeping body of the Great Lady of the Night back down into the darkness from where we came. Hine-nui-te-pō is waiting to welcome us home, waiting to embrace us so that new life can be born again.

Hine is a sacred and living goddess in Māori culture. Across Polynesia there are many goddesses called Hine, often with different endings to their names, and different manifestations. Hine appears as maiden, mother, creator. Each has her own sacred stories, rituals and particular powers.

Fortuna

Roman

She raises you up, there's wine in your cup when Fortuna turns her wheel. She plunges you low, there's nothing but woe as Fortuna spins her wheel. Her wheel is spinning round and round and round. Her wheel is turning upside down.

The Goddess Fortuna governs fate. She stands beside her celestial wheel and turns it while we sleep. Fortuna can appear as a young maiden or an old crone, but her eyes are always bound with a cloth. Fortuna is blind and does not know what fate she brings us, good or bad. She cannot see and does not mind which way her wheel turns. At the top of her wheel is bounty and abundance, at the bottom pain and suffering. But she turns her wheel impartially.

As the Goddess Fortuna turns our lives, she turns too, changing from old to young and back again. Fortuna manifests as all the mighty goddesses in one. Fortuna Primigenia is the first one, the original creator. Fortuna Virgo protects virgins.

Fortuna Dubis is doubtful fate, giving crazed courage to poor warriors who have no escape. Fortuna Virilis increases sexual power. Fortuna Respiciens is a mother who provides for all. Fortuna Redux steers the return, guiding all journeys back to their end.

Will this be my day, will things go my way when Fortuna turns her wheel? Her wheel is spinning round and round and round. Her wheel is turning upside down.

Can we influence Lady Luck? Can we change fickle fortune and the fate she spins for us? The Goddess Fortuna loves perfume. Burn frankincense and let the fragrant smoke spiral up to heaven. Fortuna might just breathe it in and be inspired to turn her wheel again. Bake her a honey cake and offer it at her shrine. She might just partake of it and in return kiss the dice, blow on the cards and turn her wheel so that you reach the very top. But if you do, know that it will not last. As the year turns, her wheel turns. As Earth turns, her wheel turns. As the planets turn, her wheel turns. Nothing is outside Fortuna's wheel. So, be like all Roman Emperors and keep a statue of the Goddess Fortuna by your bed. She might be holding her wheel, riding a horse, carrying a rudder or a cornucopia filled with gold, but she is always blindfolded. Whisper her hymns and prayers every night, be grateful for all she has given you, thank her for your life as you fall asleep and bless her as you wake. Then she might just keep her wheel turning.

Look out for Fortuna in European fairy tales where heroes and heroines search for her to change their fate, and in doing so change her too.

Cihuacóatl,
Snake Woman

Aztec, Mexico

The Eternal Grandmother is so ancient her skin has worn away. Her head is a skull with a few strands of stringy hair. Her body a thin bag of rattling bones. But she has not lost her power. The crone Cihuacóatl is still a ruthless warrior.

It was she who invented war. She who created shields, shaped spears, forged knives. If Cihuacóatl gives you one of her weapons, you will be blessed. She appears on the edge of the battlefield wearing a skirt of deadly green snakes and a crown of obsidian knives and fills the air with terrifying cries. When the battle is over, Snake Woman walks through the night, dishevelled, weeping for the dead and calling them to come to her. Cihuacóatl becomes the Goddess of Death and her cries are irresistible. Her victims have no choice and appear before her in a trance. Her bony jaw opens and she devours the dying. Her skeleton mouth is the gateway to death and she takes each soul down into her black tomb. There the Goddess of Death grinds up bones, shakes her skirt of green snakes and the souls are born again.

The Goddess of Death is a fierce mother who gives birth to the next generation. The Eternal Grandmother protects women in labour, offering them her shield and spear. Giving birth is going into battle, childbirth is war and Cihuacóatl gives women courage. She helps them fill the air with cries and cuts the cord with her obsidian knife. Her black tomb is really a womb and she is the gateway to life. When a child is born, Cihuacóatl shakes her skirt of snakes, stamps her feet and dances for joy. The snakes slough off their skin and the Eternal Grandmother grows young again. Plump flesh covers her bones, her hair grows thick and lustrous and her black tomb turns green, an arbour covered in flowers. Snake Woman shows us how to live and live again. The Goddess of Death is the gateway to eternal life.

Cihuacóatl is the patron of midwives. You can find more myths about her where she appears as a creator, and mother of the god Mixcoatl, who she lost and then filled a lake with tears of sorrow. There are also many legends of her appearing miraculously to ordinary people.

Cailleach

Ireland

The old hag will outlive us all.

Cailleach has long, white hair covered in a caille, a veil that hides many secrets. Her back is bent and she leans on a staff of twisted oak. She collects stones and rocks, gathering them into her apron. She shakes her apron and stones fall to the ground, turning into mountains. She strikes two stones together with a loud crack, waking us up, warning us to take care of her earth. If she lifts her caille you will see her face is dark blue, her teeth red and she only has one eye in the middle of her forehead. Don't scream, do not make a sound. If she sees you, she will shake her staff, cold winds will blow, snow will fall and your lips will turn blue. But on the first of February, Saint Brigid's Day, spring comes and Cailleach begins to lose her power. She fights, bringing frosts until the first of May, Beltane, then Cailleach finally lays down her staff beneath a holly bush. Some say she shrinks and shrinks, turns cold and hard and becomes a stone. Others say a crack appears in a rock and she slips through. She disappears into the earth, goes down deep inside a mountain. And there she stays all summer. But she is not alone. She has countless husbands. Each husband living a long life, each dying of old age.

Cailleach outlives them all, marrying again and again, there is no shortage of husbands! But on the thirty-first of October, Samhain, she returns. The blue-faced spook emerges from the earth for Halloween. The veiled fright picks up her staff and everything runs. Humans, animals, even plants hide as Cailleach shakes her staff and spreads snow.

How does the old hag seduce her husbands? Beneath the veil Cailleach is not what she seems. You might find her shrouded in her veil sitting by a fresh water spring. That is where the king's four sons found her. They were looking for water. It had not rained for more than a year. Their kingdom had dried up and become a barren wasteland. The king's sons set out, one after the other to find water. The eldest son, Fergus, found a spring bubbling up from underground and an old woman guarding it. She spoke through a veil, 'Kiss me and you may drink.'

Fergus lifted her caille and saw a blue face, red teeth and one eye! Fergus turned and ran for his life. The old woman cried, 'Piss for no kiss.'

The kingdom remained barren.

The next son, Ailill, raised the veil, groaned and ran.

'Piss for no kiss!' she called after him.

There was no water and nothing grew.

Fiachrae, the third son, steeled himself and gave the hag a quick peck on her whiskered cheek.

'Drip for a lip,' she said.

A trickle of water appeared in a dry river bed.

The youngest son, Niall, bowed to the crone, 'I will kiss you and do more.'

He lifted the caille, took her wrinkled hands in his, embraced her and kissed her full on the mouth. Her bony body softened, her white hair turned black, her lips became full and rosy and two dark eyes appeared. The old hag became a young and lovely maiden.

'Who are you?' asked Niall.

'I am Sovereignty. Mother of the Land. I am the source. Now you have embraced the mother, water and land are yours.'

Rain fell, water flowed, filling rivers and wells. The kingdom was green at last. And with the blessing of Sovereignty, Niall became High King of Ireland. A drop of sovereignty went to Fiachrae for kissing the hag's cheek, and he always stood beside the King's throne.

When Niall was an old man he was walking in the mountains and came to a spring bubbling up from underground. Guarding it was a young maiden with dark eyes and rosy lips.

'Do I know you?' he asked.

'Drink!' she said and held out her hand.

Niall sat beside her and she cupped water and lifted it to his lips. He kissed her fingertips and she wrapped her arms around his neck. He pressed his lips against her warm mouth and she took his hand and placed it against her breast.

'Now you have embraced the mother,' she said 'you have returned to the source.'

Her hair began to turn white, her face blue, her teeth red and her dark eyes fused into a single eye in the centre of her forehead. She threw a veil over her face and shook a staff. Niall began to shiver violently, his lips turned blue and he fell to the ground cold, stone dead. Cailleach placed rocks around his body as a royal tomb.

'You honoured Sovereignty. And so your ancestors will rule this land for twenty-six generations after you.'

Then Cailleach bent and picked up two stones and struck them together hard. The sound echoed through the hills:

'Take care of my land!'

Cailleach has various epithets, forms and stories and is found in Scots, Irish and Manx mythologies and landscapes. Many hills, crags and mountains are named for her. Often her stories describe the battle between winter and spring and the link between land, female power and sovereignty.

Elli, Old Age

Norse

Elli is tiny, wrinkled as a nut and nearly blind. Her back is bent double and she hobbles with a stick. Thin wisps of white hair cover her head like the fluff of a dandelion. Elli is the Goddess of Old Age and is so frail she looks as if she could be blown away. She totters about inside a vast palace as big as a mountain. It needs to be big because it is a place of wonders. Old Age lives with other elemental spirits that are the forces of life. Her palace is the abode of: Fire; Ocean; Thought swifter than wind; the monstrous Midgard Serpent who encircles the world keeping it spinning, and the towering giants who hold up the sky. This place is not what it seems, and anyone who arrives here, gods, humans, beasts, are tested.

When Thor arrived he was hungry. Thor, God of Thunder, had red hair, red beard, blazing eyes, deafening voice and a huge appetite. He always carried his mighty hammer, Mjolnir, with him, it protected the gods and could bring the dead back to life. Thor was so strong he could wrestle anyone to the ground and sorted out every problem by fighting. Around his waist he wore a magic belt and if he tightened this belt it made him even stronger.

Thor stepped into the mountainous palace and bellowed, 'I AM HUNGRY!'

Elli staggered towards him on her stick and said in a shaky voice, 'If you want to eat then you must fight me first.'

Thor roared with laughter, 'You want to fight with me! An old woman challenges the great Thor to a wrestling match?'

Elli nodded her white head, threw down her stick and grabbed Thor's legs. Thor reached down to push the old woman away and Elli stood firm. Thor grabbed the old woman's slender shoulders to flip her to the ground, but Elli would not move. She gripped onto Thor's giant legs like a vice. Thor pushed back hard and nothing shifted, it was as if he was pressing against a mountain. The old woman did not even tremble. Thor tightened his belt, no one defeated him! He seized Elli under the arms to lift her feeble body from the ground but the old woman was unmoveable, her feet seemed to have roots buried deep in the earth. Elli pushed back with such force that Thor's legs wobbled. She kept on pushing and Thor's knees buckled. Elli pressed down and down and Thor's knee gave way. Elli forced Thor's knee to the ground. The old woman had won!

Thor's ruddy face went pale, his eyes grew wide, he stared at the old woman and said, 'Who are you?'

'I look weak, but no one can overcome me. Not even you. I am a goddess and all are weak before me. I am Old Age and everyone meets me in the end. I topple all. No one can withstand me. Frail and feeble, I am stronger than all of you! So don't judge anyone by the way they look, especially the elderly, they are stronger than you think.'

Elli picked up her stick and pointed at Thor, 'Don't be too downhearted, I only got you down on one knee!' And as she hobbled off, she murmured, 'Bring Thor supper, and fill the table, he's hungry!'

Hekate, Goddess
of the Three Ways

Greece

'You can't see me. I stand at the junction of three roads. You hear a creak, a hoot and look round nervously. No one is there. But I am standing close by. In my hand I hold a key. If only you would ask, I will show you the way. Say my name and I will light my torches and illuminate the best path for you to take. Leave a honey cake on the stone beside the track and I will unlock the door.'

Hekate is a wandering goddess, straying through forests and down lonely paths with her dog at her side. They love to walk in the dark together, visiting graveyards, waiting at the crossroads, lingering in doorways. No one recognises the goddess as she stands at the back of the funeral procession guiding the souls of the dead, making sure ghosts do not get lost. Wrapped in a cloak, she slips unnoticed into rooms where women cry out in the pangs of birth. She soothes their pain and rocks the cradle. She is the ignored old woman sitting by the fireplace grinding seeds and roots in a pestle and mortar. She mixes herbs in a blackened cooking pot, ready to advise which plants will heal and which will destroy, if anyone asks. This overlooked old woman is the Goddess Hekate. She has power over the three realms, heaven, earth and underworld. And her faithful dog is really a Trojan queen saved from death and transformed forever.

'Call me She Who Bears Light, She Who Serves, She Who Turns Away, She Who Stands Before The Gate. Call me Goddess of the Three Ways. My names honour the wisdom of wandering in the dark, they honour ancient female knowledge of the passage of time.'

The goddess leaves no traces, has no lovers and no children. No one is sure of her origins. Her parents might be Titans, gods, nymphs or Night itself. In her true form she might wear a shimmering silver headdress, or a crown of serpents coiling though branches of oak.

She might appear with three heads, one looking up at heaven, another looking across wide earth, a third looking down into the underworld. She might have six hands to carry her torches, axe, herbs, knife, keys. Hekate is a household goddess and grand temples are not for her. Local shrines were kept at sacred spots, entrances to a city, beside doorways. There, private rituals and intimate prayers were offered to the goddess, so Hecate might hold up her torches and illuminate the path ahead.

'You will find me at the Tri Via, the place where three roads meet. I do not bless the roads but the journey of life itself. Call me Hekate Trivia. Take care when you say this charmed word as it has come to mean something quite different. Trivia is now linked with what is lowest, least important, trivial. But Tri Via are the choices you make, and you will lose your way without my direction. I am the three in one, maiden, mother, crone. Three is me. Meet me at the Tri Via at the three phases of the moon – dark, full, new. I am always there. My three heads see all at once, the dark past, the full present, the new future. I am the true Queen of the Night. Howl my name in the city. I will see you at the crossroads.'

Hekate's image appears on gems, seals, pots, stela, gravestones. Sometimes she has three heads, or wings, or six arms. Sometimes she is with a dog, or a snake, or rides a horse. She appears as a shadowy figure in the myths of others, as a guide, healer, magician. You can find her in this collection in the myth of 'Demeter and Persephone' where the three-in-one goddess appears as three separate and mighty goddesses, maiden, mother and crone.

Bibliography

Alpers, Antony, *Maori Myths and Tribal Legends*, Longman Paul, 1964.

Benard, Elisabeth, Moon, Beverly, *Goddesses who Rule*, Oxford University Press, 2000.

Bierhorst, John, *Latin American Folktales, Stories from Hispanic and Indian traditions*, Pantheon Fairy Tale and Folklore Library, 2002.

Campbell, Joseph, Rossi, Safron (ed.), *Goddesses: Mysteries of the Feminine Divine*, New World Library, 2013.

Cashford, Jules, Baring, Anne, *The Myth of the Goddess: Evolution of an Image*, Arkana, 1991.

Durdin-Robertson, Lawrence, *A Year of the Goddess*, Bycornute Books, 1990.

Ellis, Jean A., *This is the Dreaming: Australian Aboriginal Legends*, Collins Dove, 1994.

Hall, Nor, *The Moon and the Virgin*, The Women's Press, 1980.

Henderson, Joseph L., Oaks, Maud, *The Wisdom of the Serpent*, Princeton University Press, 1990.

Gimbutas, Marija, *The Goddess and Gods of Old Europe*, Thames and Hudson, 1974.

Jackson, Guida M., *Traditional Epics*, Oxford University Press, 1994.

Johnson, Buffie, *Lady of the Beasts*, Harper Collins, 1988.

Jordan, Michael, *Myths of the World*, Kyle Cathie, 1993.

Kali, Devadatta, *In Praise of the Goddess*, Nicolas-Hays, 2003.

Knapp, L. Bettina, *Women in Myth*, State University of New York Press, 1997.

Koltuv, Barbara Black, *The Book of Lilith*, Hays, 1986.

Larrington, Carolyne (ed.), *The Feminist Companion to Mythology*, Pandora Press, 1992.

Luke, Helen. M., *Women, Earth and Spirit: The Feminine in Symbol and Myth,* The Crossroad Publishing Company, 1987.

McCrickard, Janet, *Eclipse of the Sun: An Investigation into Sun and Moon Myths*, Gothic Image Publications, 1990.

Murrell, Nathaniel Samuel, *Afro-Caribbean Religions: An Introduction to Their Historical, Cultural, and Sacred Traditions*, Temple University Press, 2010.

Perera, Sylvia Brinton, *Descent to the Goddess*, Inner City Books, 1984.

Scheub, Harold, *A Dictionary of African Mythology: The Mythmaker as Storyteller*, Oxford University Press, 2000.

Sproul, Barbara C., *Primal Myths: Creating the World*, Rider, 1979.

Warner, Marina, *Alone of All Her Sex: The Myth and Cult of the Virgin Mary*, Weidenfeld & Nicolson, 1976.

Walker, Barbara G., *The Women's Encyclopedia of Myths and Secrets*, Harper Collins, 1983.

Weigle, Marta, *Creation and Procreation: Feminist Reflections on Mythologies of Cosmogony and Parturition*, University of Pennsylvania Press, 1989.

Wilde, Lyn Webster, *On the Trail of the Women Warriors*, Constable and Co., 1999.

Wolkstein, Diane, Kramer, Samuel Noah, *Inanna: Queen of Heaven and Earth: Her Stories and Hymns from Sumer,* Harper Perennial, 1983.

Acknowledgements

Thank you to: Laura Simms for a million mighty conversations that still continue to unravel myth and female archetypes, and for your radiant performances; Lyn Webster Wilde for radical work on goddesses; Hugh Lupton and Eric Maddern for their deep and wide-ranging Goddess Retreat at Tŷ Newydd National Writing Centre of Wales in 2019, it was an inspiration; Tŷ Newydd for their bursary to attend the retreat; the many female storytellers, goddesses all, whose courageous and ground-breaking work has led the way, inspired and helped me, some of whom are no longer with us but they remain within me – Diane Wolkstein, Vi Hilbert, Betsy Whyte, Sheila Stewart, Grace Hallworth, Beulah Candappa, Marit Jerstad, Muriel Bloch, Praline Gay-Para, Ritu Verma, Georgiana Keable, Ulzhan Baibussynova, Pamela Marre, Manya Maratou, Sharon Jacksties, Jan Blake, Xanthe Gresham Knight, Heidi Dahlsveen; all the museums that hold images of the goddess; all the audiences who helped shape these versions; all the venues, storytelling clubs and festivals who have hosted storytelling performances for adult audiences – may you continue; Ben Haggarty and Kate Norgate of the Crick Crack Club, who have supported and encouraged so many of my performances; Stephe Harrop for championing female storytellers; Nicola Guy at The History Press for patiently nurturing this book; Carolyne Larrington, whose brilliant *The Feminist Companion to Mythology* has been my companion throughout; Sophie Herxheimer for our many collaborations sharing female archetypes, and Fotis for thrilling trips to secret temples and landscapes – thank you all.

Thank you for helping to make The Mighty Goddess

This book was created with mighty support from a crowdfunding campaign. Massive thanks to: Raya Ahmed; Sue Bailey; Mary Barnes; Tanya Batt; Fotios Begklis; Roumyana P. Benedict; Lesley Bennett; Eloise Birnam-Wood; Blackpine Adventure Company; BookArt Bookshop; Chris Bostock; Andy Brereton; Simon Brooks; Jenny Brown; Sara Burnett; Patrick Cahn; Sarah Campbell; Paula Carter; Katy Cawkwell; Helen Chadwick; S Chen; Jaime Churchill; Emma Clare; Joan and Peter Clayton; Tracey Collins; Fiona Collins; Philippa Cornforth; Laura K Deal; Sarah Deco; Mo Docherty; Suzie Doncaster; Rhoda Evans; April Dyer Flood; Marian Galton; Pamela Gaunt; Panos Ghikas; Jane Gottesman; Aude Gotto; Vartoug Gulbenkian; Amin Hassanzadeh Sharif;

Charlotte Herxheimer; Cecilia Hewett; Claire Hope; Belinda Hopkins; William Horder; Georgia Iliopoulou; Janet; Sharon Jacksties; Tom Jenks; Sianed Jones; Jude; Kate; Flo Klein; Laura Kling; Kate Kneale; Ania Kozaczuk; Toni Lazarou; Marion Leeper; Hugh Lupton; Eric Maddern; Iliana Magiati; Dale Mathers; Klarissa May; Heather McTague; Bailey Meeker; Clare Murphy; Kate O'Connell; Pat O'Connell; Rachel O'Leary; Andrea Reece; Dawn Rose; Rachel Rose Reid; Graeme Rigby; Meg Peppin; Clare Pollard; Ellis Pratt; Sandra; Tracy Satchwill; Nazli Tahvili; Maura Vazakas; Arnau Vilardebò; Andrew Walker; Naomi Wilds; Ruth Williams; Wiskey; Vanessa Woolf; Esther Zimmermann.